D1430928

RICHARD HILLARY

Books by Lovat Dickson

HALF BREED

OUT OF THE WEST LAND

RICHARD HILLARY
From the portrait by Eric Kennington

RICHARD HILLARY

by

LOVAT DICKSON

LONDON
MACMILLAN & CO. LTD
1950

PRINTED IN GREAT BRITAIN

TO TWO GENERATIONS

RICHARD'S

AND

JONATHAN'S

★

They are Most Rightly Reputed
Valiant, Who Though They Perfectly
Apprehend Both What is Dangerous and
What is Easie, are Never the More
Thereby Diverted From Adventuring

Thucydides, Book II, Chapter 40
(THOMAS HOBBES's translation)

From the Memorial to
Andrew Comyn Irvine at Shrewsbury School

PREFACE

I FEAR it will be asked by many who have read *The Last Enemy*, why anyone should write a life of Richard Hillary when presumably all that he wanted to record of his own thoughts and experiences is in that book. There are reasons, and I should like to be allowed to put them briefly in this prefatory note.

When Richard was killed in January 1943, it seemed to a number of us who had known him well, and who had been witnesses of the psychological struggle that was to lead him to his death, that some memorial of his brief and ardent life should be provided ; and we were conscious of a symbolism in the course of his life, and the manner and the time of his death, which was of such wide significance as to justify the project.

It was proposed first that Eric Linklater, Arthur Koestler, Phyllis Bottome, myself, and a few others who had known him intimately, should contribute essays to a memorial volume. This plan was not eventually followed, for we were all too much separated by the war. But at least two of the contributions which would have appeared in that volume have been published : Eric Linklater's "Richard

Hillary", which is included in his volume of essays, *The Art of Adventure*, and Arthur Koestler's "Man or Myth", which originally appeared in *Horizon* for April 1944, and was subsequently published in *The Yogi and the Commissar*.

That perhaps was enough. Beyond what Richard had written himself, there was little more to say; merely the anecdotes of youth, and passages from those moving and passionate letters he wrote in the last months of his life. To make a book of these fragments seemed pretentious. And yet — how shall I put it? — the memory of Richard Hillary persisted with me, and I could not help writing his story.

I have said that Richard's life seemed to us to have a symbolism for the years in which we live. Koestler's definition of this, while profound and stimulating, is not one that everybody would care to accept. For the hundreds of thousands of readers of *The Last Enemy* [1] Richard symbolized the beauty and courage and nobility of youth. He was, in fact, what many of us had only hoped to be. Proust says somewhere that when we are older the ghosts of the children that we once were come to trouble us. The ghost of mine troubled me, whenever I thought of Richard Hillary, and I could only appease it by re-creating,

[1] As a matter of interest the English edition of *The Last Enemy* has sold over 135,000 copies, the American edition 15,000, the French 35,000. The book has been translated into every European language, and is much admired in post-war Germany.

in his childhood and brief youth, the bright-eyed, the witty, the virile boy whom I had come to love.

I set out this truth without shame because I believe that for others too what that noble and tragic figure in *The Last Enemy* symbolizes is the best that boyhood and manhood can be. It seemed then allowable that I should add to the account he himself gave of his few adult years, and to the analyses of character which Eric Linklater and Arthur Koestler had so skilfully provided, the fond memories of his friends and family, and the account, taken from his diary and letters, of the last and fatal task he took on himself.

These then are to be thanked for the help they have given me, the material they have put at my disposal and the pains they have taken to provide me with all the facts I needed. First, of course, Mr. and Mrs. Michael Hillary, who have put in my hands all Richard's letters and diaries ; Mrs. Geoffrey Patterson ; Mrs. Michael Burn ; Eric Kennington, whose portrait of Richard I reproduce ; Miss Netta Demetriadi ; Mrs. Beryl Malin ; the Rev. Arthur and Mrs. Hope ; Squadron-Leader F. B. Sutton, D.F.C. ; Arthur Koestler, who had a dynamic effect on Richard's mind ; and finally, Eric Linklater, whose advice and encouragement have meant so much to me, as his friendship has during these last twenty years.

LOVAT DICKSON

LONDON, *June* 1950

LIST OF ILLUSTRATIONS

Chapter One

KING'S CROSS on a November morning in 1942. The platform for the ten o'clock train to Berwick is thronged. Dust, blown up from the empty tracks and the unswept stone platforms, gets in the eyes, and the nose stings with the sulphurous fumes of smoke, the acrid scent of corridors and of carriages that have been used too much and cleaned too seldom. Thick china cups, stained with old tea, are stacked here and there with painful neatness, and tea-wagons, mounted with nickel urns and piled with yellow buns, are pushed slowly along the crowded platform. Tea, dust, smoke, smell, the hiss of escaping steam, and the ceaseless clattering of army boots, are characteristic of the platforms of King's Cross all through the day. But at ten o'clock in the morning they rise to a crescendo of noise, to a vast funnel of odour.

Everywhere there are uniforms, khaki predominating, but Air Force blue considerably in evidence, for this line passes through Grantham and the flat fen country, where the bomber squadrons, pointing towards Germany, are hunched down amid the winter fields.

The war has been going on for three years, and its discomforts have become habitual. The platform has been crowded for the last three-quarters of an hour. Almost from the moment the train drew in every place has been taken, and the corridors are already filled with those who have despaired of finding a seat, and have settled down on kitbag and haversack.

The faces are like pale discs in the grey light of this November morning. There are faces tired and drawn from hectic leaves, and faces young and soft still with the contours of boyhood, leaving home for the first time. There are faces from every type of family and from every social background. There are village boys, and boys from country towns, sharp, pinched faces from the industrial areas, red faces from the fields, faces fresh from school; and older faces, those of men who have had years of settled, civilian life before the war drew them into its vortex. Here they are, at a point of departure, going back to camp and flying-field, or to the little ships in the ports up and down the East Coast. Milling along the platform, in and out of carriage doors, stepping over the legs of others, calling to one another, restless, noisy, poised upon the edge of departure into the various adventures of war-time life.

Only a few minutes before the train was due to

depart on this dull morning a young Air Force officer, and an older man who was plainly his father, walked up the platform, vainly yet with something of an air of ironic indifference looking for a seat. The officer was tall and well-built. He wore his peaked cap a little on one side of his head, and had his hands thrust into the pockets of his greatcoat. His figure, and the way he walked, gave the quick impression, to anyone who chanced to observe him, that he was an athlete, and the eyes of the observer moved quickly to his face, expecting to see there the freshness and youthfulness that his jaunty appearance and the elegance of his figure suggested. But most of those who glanced at it looked quickly away again out of sudden delicacy. The cold morning air brought out the weals and scars of bad burns, and the sardonic grin which he was wearing at this moment, in contemplation of his father's fussiness over being late for trains, accentuated the thin straight line of the lips which a surgeon's knife had built up out of other tissue.

There was no place to be found empty in the train, but the porter carrying his bag edged his way into the corridor of a first-class carriage, and the officer climbed in, leant out of the open window, and smiled down at the figure below.

" So long, Farve. Don't worry, I'll get a seat before long."

The face looking up at him was full of solicitude,

but the voice, when it spoke, was impatient.

"If you have to go back, God knows you might try and do it comfortably."

Richard Hillary grinned down at his father.

"Look after Mother. I'll look after myself."

Michael Hillary thought what a damned world it was, pressed his son's hand and turned away. As he walked quickly down the platform, hurrying to get to his office, a sense of his son's nobility of character, and of his own inadequacy, displayed itself to him. He might never see the boy again, and that had been no way to say goodbye. He stood irresolute. If he were to go back, he would not be able to find the words to express all the emotion that was tearing at his heart; it had never been possible to say what he really felt. Opposite where he was standing was a cigarette kiosk. He went over and bought a packet of cigarettes, turned back along the platform, found Richard still leaning through the window, thrust the cigarettes into his hand with a muttered goodbye, and walked quickly away to the station exit.

*

As the train pulled out of King's Cross, Richard Hillary stood in the passage, clutching in his skeleton-like fingers the packet of cigarettes his father had thrust at him, thinking how dear his parents were to him, and how inadequately he had repaid all their sacrifice for him. He knew what he had cost them in pleasures foregone, what anxious calculations it had taken to keep him at Shrewsbury and then at Trinity. The income of even a senior civil servant did not run to luxurious living and to the easy maintenance of a son at Public School and University. Their stint he might now have been repaying had it not been for the war. Instead, he had gone into the Service, and ever since the Battle of Britain he had provided continual anxiety for them. Because he had so painfully survived his crash, his mother had watched a protracted death instead of sustaining the sudden blow and recovering from it. And when slowly he had struggled back to life, and the weight of anxiety had been lifted, he had clamped it back with his own hands by his decision to return to active fighting. Richard knew what a blow that had been to his parents. He had had to tell his mother, and had watched the sombre look settle on her face. But the decision to go was something that he could not fight against ; a decision so merciless to her was unrelenting to him.

When the posting had come to a night fighter training unit in Berwickshire, there had been little time for remorse. He had had one evening with his parents ; then this grey November morning, his father seeing him off, this crowded corridor, and the winter fields of Hertfordshire slipping by, while the train with even breath drew him swiftly towards the North, to his ultimate fate.

*

It had ever been a parting like this, Michael Hillary thought, as he hurried away from the station. A cruel, sudden tearing apart, very painful, but not so difficult to endure as a sentimental farewell. Memory recalled to him at this moment a score of occasions when he had had to turn his back on the appealing face of his son, surrendering him to alien authority ; to his Preparatory School, then to Shrewsbury each autumn when at the end of his summer leave he and Edwyna had had to return to the Sudan ; to Oxford, and then to the R.A.F. The face of his son, which had been tear-drenched at partings before prep. school, which time, training and tradition had inured to become sombre and set as they parted each year at Shrewsbury, had with the years grown more firm, though not less sad, in dealing with these moments. But never had it seemed so unconsciously forlorn as it had at the carriage window that morning.

Every man at middle age has moments when he longs that life could begin again, not that it might then take a different and happier course, but because the remembered landscapes of earlier life are lit with such sunshine. It seems impossible that one then had had troubles and anxieties ; if they existed at all, they were small and few. Time had not run a sufficient course to gather a quantity of them. But happiness ; why, happiness on the other hand was then something still unspent ; an accumulation at one's disposal. The years are a heavy drain on it, and there may come a time when one is bankrupt. At this moment Michael Hillary felt that he and Edwyna, parting from Richard a second time in the war, had exhausted their balance. What remained but a repetition of the agonizing suspense they had already endured ; and at some dread moment, the swift pain that would flash to the heart even as they took in from the door the Air Ministry telegram, and then the long dull purposelessness of living out their time ?

It must have seemed to Michael Hillary on that grey November morning, coming from saying a second farewell to his son in this war, a damned and hideous world, but I am sure that nothing in his swift gait, the thrown-back shoulders and the square-cut soldierly face indicated the sombre nature of his thoughts as he left King's Cross and, swinging his neatly-rolled umbrella, made his way to his office.

Chapter Two

LOOKING back to that grey morning of the war, and at that ravaged but still golden young man, going with sardonic wilfulness towards his death, it is possible to glimpse both the plight of our age and something of the dour courage with which the majority of people have met its misfortunes. In Richard Hillary's young life, and slow and bitter death, there seems indeed something symbolic of the stretched, protracted agony through which mankind is passing, and it is that which gives a special significance to an account of his life.

Here is a young man who was born in 1919, after the first great war, and who was killed in the middle of the second great war at the age of twenty-three. All the life that he had known had been spent at Public School and University, in training camp and in combat. He was no different from a great many of his fellows, save that he had an exceptionally observant eye, and a quick, eager curiosity about the meaning of life. The war, when it came, seemed to him, as it did to so many others, not a vast and solemn dispute about liberty or territories, not a test as to whether man was to be free or enslaved, but a great and vivid adventure. His generation did not, like Rupert Brooke's, declaim that " God be thanked that He had matched them with this hour ", but went instead, flushed with excitement and the more eager because of the long, tedious waiting, to match themselves with other youths of a foreign land who had been overweening, insulting, and the most God-awful bullies and bores. Impatiently, and with glorious confidence, they leapt into action, and withstood the heavy shock of the attack, as Drake's captains had done when the Armada sailed ponderously into the English Channel.

Churchill's words, and these youths, saved England at a pinch ; and when the first shock of battle was over, Richard Hillary, like countless others, was maimed and lay in hospital. It is possible, and brave, and fine, to go singing into battle, but after battle, lying in a hospital bed, only those in delirium sing. This boy lay there month after month, while the surgeons ceaselessly laid patch after patch upon him, to make him presentable to humankind again ; and while they worked he thought. And when the surgeons had finished and he came back into the world again, he wrote a book, *The Last Enemy*, which expressed simply but ardently all that his generation felt. Such a book might have been written by one of Drake's lieutenants, if books had been as plentiful in those days, to tell what a man felt after grappling with the high Spanish ships, seeing his friends killed, and coming back to the lee of Plymouth shore again.

In *The Last Enemy* Richard spoke not only for England but for the youth of all the free countries of the world. Year after year through the war, and ever since, thousands of copies of this book have been bought. Already in England it has sold 135,000 copies. It has been translated into every European language. To-day in the universities of Western Europe, from Norway down to France, the young men who were his contemporaries in age, though of a different nation, write theses for their degrees on Richard Hillary, and those that I have seen are always concerned with some evaluation of him as representative of the youth of the world. Indeed, this seems the most moving memorial that has been erected to his young life, that after the tide of German occupation had rolled back from the countries of Western Europe, and it was possible again for young men to pursue knowledge, the generation who had fought, whether in freedom or under cover and the threat of execution, turning to books again, so often chose to study the life of Richard Hillary, the exemplar of what mankind has suffered and aspired to in these painful years of man's perpetual struggle. In his happy beginning, who would have imagined such a destiny for him?

★

Richard Hillary

Richard was born in Sydney, Australia, on April 20th, 1919. His father, Michael Hillary, had been in government service in Melbourne, and a few months before the first war broke out had married Edwyna Hope, who came from North-Western Australia. Both Michael and Edwyna Hillary were Australian, Michael of Anglo-Irish descent, Edwyna of Scottish and Spanish descent. Michael Hillary had joined the Army soon after the outbreak of war, protesting and overcoming, as his son was to do twenty-two years later, some official bar to service on the grounds, in his case, of defective eyesight. He had served in India and Mesopotamia. In 1918 he was given leave, and returned to Australia for three months. In September of that year he had left again for the Middle East, and by a fortunate coincidence returned to Sydney after the war on the night his son, Richard, was born.

On his discharge from the Army, Michael Hillary went into the government service again. He took a small flat in South Yarra, and later a house in Toorak, and here Richard spent the first three years of his life.

The portrait of Richard in childhood must be recreated largely from knowing what he was like as a young man. The wavering lines of the boy's personality may be brought a little more into focus by the addition of some anecdotes and recollections from family sources. These appear at first sight to be of a contradictory nature, but on investigation the contradictions are explained. Lively boys have more than one side to their nature, and children with a reputation for perfection of behaviour do not usually make interesting subjects as adults. His Aunt Beryl, Edwyna Hillary's sister, remembers him at this time. "It was noticeable," she says, "that he had a good head, fine vivid blue eyes, a ridiculous nose and a large mouth, and a tendency to pout his lower lip. When grieved, he had a habit of screwing his eyes tightly shut, opening his mouth wide, and letting the tears pour down into his mouth without let or hindrance." The picture of Richard that emerges is that of an ordinary boy with a somewhat aggressive cast of face, very lithe and active, and inclined to be self-assertive in his opinions. His father's Irish ancestry was preserved in his temper ; the indubitable promise of his good looks was an inheritance from his mother. His Aunt Beryl recalls that he was capable of getting literally hopping mad, looking the very embodiment of a small fury. The outbreak would quickly spend itself, though sometimes he would remain petulant until he would realize how comic his sulky face looked, and he would as quickly burst into laughter. This rare and precious quality of being able to see the ridiculous in himself never deserted him. But it grew sharper, more pointed, perhaps too embracing as he grew older, as he observed with that clear, honest unflinching gaze of his the ridiculous aspect in others. Comments leap at me from the pages of his diary ; sharp, acid, derisory, the pointed barbs he used to satisfy his anger when he was a man and had learnt to control his temper, but still felt it surge within him.

The crossing of Irish, Spanish and Australian blood, in fact, had produced a lively and attractive boy, with a quick, volatile nature, which was manifested in his habit of sticking out his lower jaw when crossed, but melting suddenly into smiles, and winning over authority to his side with a sudden flowering of charm that was quite irresistible. His aunts, his uncle and his parents' friends remember that he was a strong little fellow, with an athletic figure and a gift for games ; but they remember that in his early years he was a bad loser. When he wanted to be charming he could overcome all opposition. When he was obstinate or difficult he could be excessively irritating.

But he was a devoted son, sure sign that his home had been a happy one. His mother was always first in his thoughts, and her good opinion meant more to him than that of anyone else. His father he regarded in a different way, so I gathered from him in talks later in his life. Secretly he admired him and his achievements ; he was the sort of father, busily remote, able to exact respect and obedience, and to stand up to the world and order his own relations with it ; the sort of father, in short, who fits a small boy's standards of perfection.

But, while it was possible to take this detached though admiring view of his father, whom he saw only at infrequent intervals, with his mother it was different. Towards her his devotion remained always utter, lasting, unquestioning and complete.

One does not have to grope for the explanation. All Richard's early years were spent in close companionship with his mother. They were together all day, while she was shopping, when she was with her friends; and more than ever when business took Michael Hillary, who had become Secretary to Billy Hughes, the Prime Minister of Australia, away from Melbourne. Their minds and their hearts became intertwined, like one root grafted on another; and on tides of domesticity, talking continually to his mother, with her every moment of the day, Richard was borne onwards in the first years of his life. There were no other children in the family, and there were no relatives in the city. Edwyna Hillary herself was a stranger to Melbourne, and the child became as much the centre of her life as she was of his. The commingling of their minds and hearts in those early years established a relationship of exceptional intimacy and understanding. It made separation later at boarding-school a suffering for them both, and in the face of death at the end the fear of giving pain to his mother was the chief thing that Richard dreaded.

EDWYNA HILLARY
From a photograph taken in 1917

A coloured photograph of Edwyna Hillary, taken soon after her marriage, shows a slender young woman, tall, graceful, with an erect carriage and a face of real freshness and beauty. From the picture look forth the blue eyes which were Richard's most striking feature ; and the skin has that smoothness and hue of health which were preserved in Richard's face even after the many applications of McIndoe's healing knife in 1940 and 1941. The photograph was taken in summer weather. A large straw hat shades the face, and a long silk dress, drawn in by a belt, emphasizes the girlish slightness of the young figure ; and its eagerness, for it seems to incline slightly forward, and the smile about the lips, seem, as one looks at it now, a first glimpse of the tense, eager figure, the teasing smile of the boy, then not born, who was always to be recalled to the memory of those who had known him in that attitude of radiant eagerness and unquenchable vitality.

But though Edwyna Hillary's devotion was intense, she did not spoil Richard. She exacted the highest standards of obedience from him, and did not hesitate to punish him for wrongdoing. Richard, on his part, expected and demanded the best from his mother. One small incident, chosen from many, will illustrate this. A larger boy, coming upon Richard and two small friends building a sand castle on the beach, took lordly delight in demolishing the work of several hours with some swift destructive kicks. Richard jumped up from his knees, his face blazing, and knocked him flat on his back where he lay bellowing. Edwyna Hillary and the boy's mother rushed up simultaneously, while with outraged cries the injured youth told the tale of Richard's dastardly attack. Richard was called upon by Mrs. Hillary to apologize both to the boy and his mother ; but mutinous, and red-faced still with anger, he refused. He said he was not sorry, and could not therefore say he was. The combined persuasion and command usual on such occasions bringing forth nothing, and the injured boy still clamant on his back, the mother observed that not only was Richard a wicked and dangerous little boy, but showed by his disobedience that he was the worst brought-up child she had ever met.

" I entirely agree with you," said Mrs. Hillary, " but what do you suggest I do ? "

The mother and the crying child, offering no answer, departed, but Richard knew no sense of triumph at having had his way about the apology. The look of mutiny turned to one of regret. A mournful cast spread over his small red face. " Am I really badly brought up ? " he asked his mother.

" I don't think you have been by me," said Mrs. Hillary, " and I've certainly met ruder boys than you."

" Oh, but, Muz, why did you say so then ? " wailed Richard.

For a long time he kept returning to the subject, and only gradually did it become clear that what worried him was not his own shortcomings in the way of being brought up, but that his mother should have said something that was not true.

It is not often enough remembered that parents are constantly being judged by their children. To what lengths will a child not go to hide from the world what it thinks to be the failings and weaknesses of those it loves, and how it suffers for their sins. On that bright summer day, so long ago now, I see in imagination those two figures walking away hand in hand from the beach, the slim young mother in her summer dress and the small boy with the golden head, trailing his bucket and spade, but weighed down more by the woe of his discovery that his mother had said something that was not true.

And I catch an echo in a letter Richard wrote to his mother much later, a few days before his death: " There are moments, far too many of them, when you make my heart turn over, and I am filled with such an unutterable tenderness for you and all you have done for me that in my happiness I feel quite sad ".

★

There is another trait to be noticed. He was constantly asking questions. This is characteristic of every intelligent child who, mystified by the world which surrounds him, hopes that grown-ups, though they sometimes appear so foolish, yet are nevertheless so wise and may have the key to the mystery. Heaven lies about us in our infancy, hardly distinguishable from the real world. When elders laugh at the naïveté of such questions, innocency is shattered for the sensitive child, and shades of the prison-house begin to close in.

They were so much alone together, and conversation had never-ending delight for both of them, though it was broken by these lacunae of misunderstanding. At such moments a chasm opened between the boy and his mother, across which he gazed at her with blue eyes large with doubt.

" I get so tired," he said one day, head propped up by his fist, " of people talking about God. Why does not someone tell me about Mrs. God ? "

" There is no Mrs. God, darling."

" No Mrs. God ! ", flabbergasted. " Then who looks after the angels and tucks them into bed like you do me ? "

" Richard, what a lovely idea ! Now, darling, let me read to you," said Mrs. Hillary hastily, dreading next some question about Jesus.

A few weeks later, Richard celebrated his birthday, and amongst the telegrams of congratulation from his relations was one signed Lillian.

" Who is Lillian ? " asked Richard.

" Your godmother."

A moment's silence, and Mrs. Hillary felt the sharp blue eyes fixed on her accusingly.

" What is it, darling ? " she asked.

"You said there was no Mrs. God, and now I've had a telegram from her."

*

A clear, unbiased view of Richard at this stage, and later in his life, is provided by Mrs. Beryl Malin. She, who had made Richard's acquaintance when he was twenty-four hours old, and had firmly refused to dote, had noted at the time " nothing special to distinguish him from his fellow creatures of similar age ". As he grew, she conceded him to be an " intelligent, mischievous, rather truculent little boy, usually cheerful and cheeky ".

Mrs. Malin's account of the growing boy is a brilliant piece of exposition of character, for it reveals — I think unconsciously as regards the writer — the quality in Richard that distinguished him from others ; his power, even when quite small, to wear down the opposition of others, to impress his personality on those reluctant to approve him. Twenty years later he was to overcome my prejudices in the same way ; and it has been satisfactory to have evidence that Mrs. Malin succumbed to a much more miniature edition of Richard than that which won me over.

Mrs. Malin notes other of his traits, in her masterly

summing-up of Richard's character. Admiration for him creeps in unawares. From " nothing special to distinguish him " at twenty-four hours old, she passes with the years to note that " he was fundamentally an honest, straightforward person, but argumentative to the *n*th degree. He was naturally impatient and intolerant. . . . He had a tremendous zest for life. . . . He did everything with gusto. . . . He was [this when he was at Oxford] a handsome, high-spirited, laughing egoist, with charm of manner."

So far had the infant child progressed, thus had the boy with " nothing special to distinguish him " become the man. But Mrs. Malin's admirable sketch has led us beyond Richard's boyhood. We must return to the family view taken of him when he was four or five.

★

The past is lit with anecdotes. How well some families remember these things. These come from aunts and uncles, as well as from his parents. Everyone was fond of him, but everyone was aware of his potentiality for mischief. The chant went up, and was sustained in the family circle : Richard is spoilt. The boy has a temper. Richard should be punished. The boy will be ruined. But each complainant was captured in turn. They continued to urge that unless a policy of severity or deprivation of some particular treat was followed, the outcome could

On arrival in England

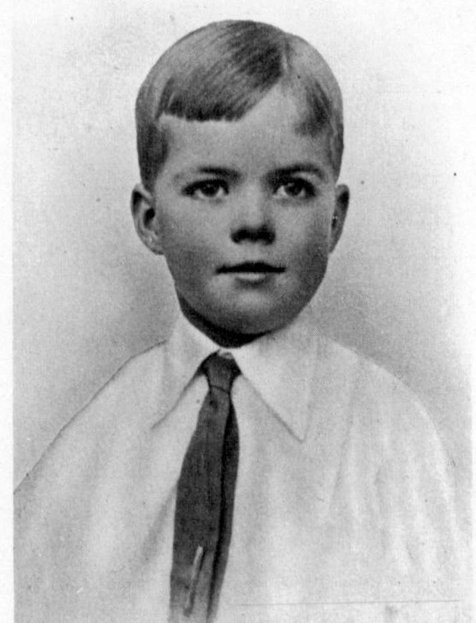

At Preparatory School

RICHARD

only be disaster ; and each, I think, was secretly of the opinion that only he or she could really handle him.

Edwyna Hillary was much too fond of her son to let transgression go unpunished. The harsh process of correction was painful to them both. Remorse, his for his sin, hers for her harshness, drew them together afterwards in the sweet pain of reconciliation. He came in time to sense her moods, her very thoughts, the images that lay shaped but unspoken behind her eyes. " Both our hearts are breaking," he cried once, when he was being left at school, flinging his arms round her and pressing his tearful face to hers, quite certain that she shared his sorrow.

It was not that he was continually in trouble, but he was ever threatening to be ; and suspense is worse than outright accident. Little Richard was growing aggressive, and he was domineering. He was extremely reckless within the scope for danger open to a small boy. His mother doted on him ; mothers are often so inclined towards their sons. But it seems to have been thought that Edwyna Hillary did not sufficiently hide it. Richard was embarrassingly direct. The young are frequently timid and shy with strangers. It boded ill that this particular boy had an unnatural air of affability, and could sometimes cause his elders embarrassment by the directness with which he put complete strangers at their ease.

*

When Richard was three Michael Hillary had the opportunity of a visit to London on a mission to Australia House. It needed only Billy Hughes' blessing — " You've never been to London ? Every man should know that city " — to persuade him to go in the first place. While he was still in England on this three years' tour of duty, an important and permanent position in the Sudan was offered to him. He accepted this, and on his first leave took a house in Beaconsfield to which they could return for holidays.

The excitement of the move to England must at first have been pleasant for Richard, satisfying to every sense and apprehension in his lively young body and mind. Adventure, movement, change, were always to be especially attractive to him. Life on board ship had proved to one of his gregarious and pleasant nature a splendid prelude to this translation, but it can be surmised that Beaconsfield at first impact was a little subduing to a violent young spirit, used to the freer ways of Australian life. He must have missed the almost limitless sandy beaches of the Pacific, where so much of his time had been spent, and the prevalent greyness of English skies must have struck a contrast in his mind, remembering the sunlit, salty air of coastal Australia.

It is on record that the bright spirit momentarily pined, and a visit was arranged to the Reverend Arthur Hope, Edwyna Hillary's brother, who at that time had a living in the Dukeries. Mr. Hope has provided an account of this first visit which illuminates Richard's character at this time.

His mother took him as far as Grantham by train. Here Mr. Hope met him. There was a sudden swift parting from his mother, the first there had ever been ; and Richard was swept off by his clerical uncle on a branch line, through Newark to Tuxford, from Tuxford by dog-cart to the vicarage, lost in the countryside of Nottinghamshire.

The picture that emerges from Mr. Hope's recollections of this visit is of a small boy, with a red face, a pair of frosty blue eyes and an exceedingly stiff upper lip, sandwiched between Uncle and Aunt in the dog-cart, impervious to their ventures at cheerfulness, but momentarily warmed to the semblance of a smile by the news that the mare was named Tavey. The brown hindquarters of Tavey, the comfortable clip-clop of her hooves, the flickering of her sensitive ears, must have been reassuring to the young exile, for Mr. Hope recalls that he gazed at her for most of the journey, suddenly cheered up, and subsequently became greatly attached to Tavey.

Mrs. Hope had been warned that Richard was " tissicky " about food at home. The Vicarage had two children of its own, healthy boys older than Richard, who were devoted to suet puddings and the other plain well-cooked dishes characteristic of the

Rectory table. The two Hope boys, Edmund and Robin, were away at boarding-school, but the table did not vary whether the boys were there or whether the Vicar was the solitary example of manhood. Richard, tired of fruit and foods acknowledged excellent for the proper functioning of the young machine, took to suet puddings with zest. His aunt records :

He was a little homesick the first night, for he was not quite six, but he soon recovered.

He soon recovered, indeed.

He was a little boy [Aunt Kate recalls] who liked to take command of the situation. If one drove with him, he would press to do the driving. One day I took him over to see the water-mill that was in our Parish, and coming home he clamoured to take the reins. And when I had given way to him, we were soon on the grass verge. " You really must give me the reins, Dick," I said — but I had to take them —

confesses Aunt Kate, and the fluster of the situation is evident in her account of it — " for it wasn't his idea at all," she concludes in the tone of one battered from the fray.

But there are softer shades in the portrait of Richard that emerges from his stay at Egmanton. He used to like being read to :

He sat as good as gold, drinking the stories in [report the affectionate uncle and aunt]. Egmanton was only a few miles from Sherwood Forest and so was practically in Robin Hood country. Edmund, away at boarding-school, had had a book about Robin Hood given him by one of his godfathers.

Out of this, Aunt Kate read to him at night, and his imagination was inflamed. But there was doubtful morality in the tale of Robin Hood, and Aunt Kate, seeking to correct it, would close the book shortly before lights-out and tell, from her own pure imagination, stories of saints and angels. "Not yet six" was the infant age with which his aunt kept crediting Richard. It is on record that he was fascinated by the Robin Hood stories, but there is no evidence of his having been enthralled by the exploits of saints and angels. Aunt Kate persisted with these inspiring tales, with which the infant mind might be reckoned to sleep sound and wholesome the night through; but I imagine, in retrospective mood, the infant Richard, head on pillow, blue eyes solemn, and small mind busy with Friar Tuck and Robin Hood, while above his head a patient kindly face extols the exploits of martyrs and saints whose blameless lives of Christian endeavour must have seemed not one-half so enviable as the outright, bluff and rude existence of Robin Hood.

This visit to the Hopes was the first of many. The night before he left to return to London, Richard confessed to Aunt Kate: "I want to live here, I want to die here, and be buried here. I don't like London and the streets."

While Aunt Kate recorded :

He loved the freedom of the country, the picnics we went, the pony and the dogs ; walks in the woods stirred his imagination, and he got a lot of fun out of them and the games that could be played.

Uncle Arthur noted :

When this holiday was over, Kate took him to King's Cross and delivered him into the hands of his mother.

One notes a certain relief in that, a lightening of tension in the atmosphere of the Rectory. But remembered later, Mr. Hope recalls only the bright image whose first visit to his Rectory this was. Richard comes again many times in the next dozen years. When he is killed, the Rector writes down his recollections, and concludes :

I am glad all this matter has been restored to my recollection ; it is like renewing my acquaintance with Dick as a child — and it has been a pleasure, as indeed was the actual intercourse of those dozen or so years when our lives touched ; for he was certainly dear to my heart.

*

Between the boy and his mother a bond already tightly meshed continued to be woven. This is to be remarked, not because it is unusual between a mother and an only son, but because it was later to stand the strain of so much separation, yet remain ever to him the light and meaning, the good, the memory of pure intent in his life. I remember that he told me, during the time of his convalescence after the Battle of Britain, that no matter at what time the parties he went to ended, he would go into his mother's room, sit on her bed, and tell her all that had happened during the day.

"Doesn't your father object to being woken up at three or four in the morning?" I asked him, presuming from his account that his mother didn't.

"Of course," he replied, with the characteristic quizzical look in his blue eyes, "but I tell him to roll over and go to sleep."

This habit of intimate exchange of thought was engendered in the early years, when they were so much alone together. But it also sprang from Richard's absolute honesty of character. Since he did nothing of which he was ashamed, at moments when others might have preserved a shy reticence the fundamental forthrightness of his character made him speak, especially to his mother. The diary he kept when he was in London after his discharge from hospital is full of references to his talks with her; his delight when, after one evening, or several, of late parties, or before his return to East Grinstead for one of the innumerable operations he had to undergo, he could spend several hours at a time with her.

She was terrified of spoiling him, and had constantly to check herself against demonstrating her affection for him too much. This led to little severities that wrung her heart, brought temporary desolation to his, then suffused them with the utter sweetness of reconciliation. Soon an occasion presented itself for testing the sacrifice that each could make for the other.

Michael Hillary was appointed Auditor-General of the Sudan, and Mrs. Hillary had to accompany him to Khartoum. Richard was now of an age to go to school. During the summer holidays various establishments were inspected, and one was selected which seemed the best. In late September, in 1926, Richard was deposited there. The excitement of going away to school had dulled the apprehension of what separation from his mother was going to mean. Not until they were in the Headmaster's study did the horror of what was about to happen come upon him. But Mrs. Hillary had taught the boy to be manly. His eyes became preternaturally bright, his face crimson, his jaw set hard, silence gripped him. She bent to kiss him, and hurried away with Michael.

Richard always remembered with hatred his years at that preparatory school. Every letter he wrote begged his mother to take him away and put him in some other establishment. With what feelings those letters were read in Khartoum can be imagined. Each summer Mrs. Hillary returned, determined to move Richard, found him healthy, happy and strong, unmarked by the scars she had anticipated in Khartoum his sufferings would have left on him. When his holidays began each year, nothing more wasteful, abhorrent and altogether senseless could be imagined by either of them than a round of visits of inspection to other schools. And when the holidays ended, it was too late to do anything. The misery had to be endured through another winter.

The weary time thus passed until that summer came when he would be returning no more to the hated place, and a preliminary visit had to be made to the Public School which had been chosen for him; where, if all went well at the Headmaster's interview, he would immure himself that coming September.

Shrewsbury had enticements to offer which the preparatory school had lacked. Shrewsbury was famous, and it was unthinkable not to be loyal to your Public School, and regard it as supreme above all others. Shrewsbury had the river, and if all was propitious he might row. Finally Shrewsbury represented the System; it provided the pattern on which a man's life had to be based. From Shrewsbury one went to University, from University into the world, and became a man. Going there was an adult, serious, responsible step.

Nevertheless, whether through secret misgivings,

or temperamental stage-fright, or whether because he was only twelve, Richard on the way to his interview behaved in a fashion which endeared him to no one. He had been told to try to make a good impression, to show himself intelligent and not forget everything that he had learned. On the way there by car, he sat in the back while his parents sat in front. He had brought with him, amongst other *aide-mémoire*, a Latin grammar, and had been droning Latin verbs over and over in a last-minute panic to commit them to memory. Suddenly the demon temperament sought expression. He shut the book with a bang.

"I'm going to hate it," he said fiercely, "I am going to hate it all."

His father and mother ignored this statement, and continued their conversation. Richard repeated it, with added loudness and fierceness, and they continued to ignore it. Whereupon Richard repeated the jingle of verbs he had just been learning, and ended : "I'm going to hate the whole place. I'm going to hate everyone there. I'm going to hate everything about it." Then the verbs again, and then this prophecy of anathema and woe ; again the verbs, again the hate, with all the maddening persistence of a small boy.

Edwyna Hillary knew her son well. What he wanted was an argument to relieve the tension of his own feelings, but she could not bring herself to debate a point so painful to her. Instead she responded to the tension with one of her occasional severities, which she always took as evidence that she did not spoil the boy.

" All right, Richard. You are going to hate everyone there, and in all probability everyone will hate you. Now for heaven's sake be quiet."

An appalled silence followed while the egoist in the back seat weighed up this unexpected possibility. When they met the Headmaster, Canon Sawyer, Richard was perfectly self-possessed. He immediately showed his liking for Sawyer, answered whatever small questions were asked him without hesitation, made a good impression on the Headmaster ; and they left Shrewsbury, happy in the belief that the future was to be different from the past.

*

He was at Mr. Whitfield's house at Shrewsbury for six years until 1937, when he left to go to Oxford. What can be said of those years ? He was happy enough, did sufficiently well both at games and in school to cut the necessary figure that makes a boy remembered in his generation, gives him pleasure at the time, and a nostalgic feeling for the place afterwards.

The Public School system is a strong one. It brings all rebels to conform. Its virtue indeed is the high state of uniformity it imprints on a myriad individuals. Richard learnt to be self-reliant, to be a good sportsman, and to be unselfish. Courage to the point of recklessness had been an attribute born in him. Shrewsbury changed it sensibly, made it unflamboyant, made self-sacrifice for a good cause seem a worthy aim, and shallow recklessness appear mere ostentation. It gave him the boon of friendship, the sense of a deep understanding with a few others. It taught him the virtue of the team-spirit, a hard lesson for someone so very individualistic to learn ; to suppress one's own desire to excel in the general urge to make one's side supreme.

Shrewsbury also awakened the possibilities that were latent in his quick, eager mind. He had always loved words, and before he could read himself, his ear would catch a word that had for him some musical or mellifluous sound. "That is a lovely word," he would say, repeating it over and over again, and he would tell his mother that it was a blue or red word, naming some colour that represented to him its particular radiance. He had become an eager, omnivorous and undiscriminating reader. And this bright mind and quick imagination were just at the point to be caught and directed by a really good teacher. Such a one, with all the necessary tact and understanding, there was at Shrewsbury in the person of Mr. McEachran. Richard confided to this master, who had lent him various books, that he wanted to become a writer, and that the model on which he wished to base himself was the American novelist, John Steinbeck. McEachran's genius was not to think this presumptuous in a fifteen-year-old boy, and instead to lead him by way of worthwhile books to an appreciation of good writing, and to encourage in him an ambition which is so often the subject of ridicule if anyone professes before attempting it. Richard was never to forget McEachran's influence. His name came up often in his talk, and once broadcasting in America, he named him as the greatest influence in his life.

Shrewsbury set its stamp upon him, but Richard was a character who could never be quite contained in any mould. His mind was too lively and critical to accept unquestioningly certain dogmas which the Public School system requires of its followers. Also his upbringing, the long separation from his parents, the many holidays he had to spend alone, the freedom that was allowed him by his parents to travel wherever he liked ; and, finally, the charm he possessed which could even unseat authority on occasion, or divert it from the proper purpose ; all these things combined to make Richard in outward appearance a nice-looking, well-brought-up young Englishman of the best class, but within an unpredictable, dynamic individual, capable alike of considerable mischief, of unrelenting obstinacy, or of unusual achievement.

Peter Pease, who was to play such a part in the ultimate shaping of Richard's character, was in the same years at Eton conforming admirably to type. Richard at Shrewsbury was conforming outwardly but within himself building up a disturbing reserve of power which the war was to release in an unexpected way. When they came to know each other, part of Richard's admiration for Peter was to see with what perfection the system could shape the product to its ends. Peter's admiration for Richard, on the other hand, was the unholy fascination of watching an illicit deviation from type, and wondering what explosive end it was to reach.

*

During this time he recorded with that frankness so characteristic of him what he meant to do with his life. He had told McEachran that he meant to be a writer, and that was no sudden whim. Though like all good writers in the making, he frequently despaired of achieving his ambition, he never contemplated the possibility of abandoning it.

He was faced with the necessity, again as writers often are, of compromising. His father, with some reason, was for justifying the large expense of educating him by entering him for a profession. To Michael Hillary there was no better profession than the one in which he himself had succeeded so well, and which offered satisfactory rewards as well as a life of considerable interest. The Sudanese Government chose its officials by personal selection. Shrewsbury and Trinity, a satisfactory scholastic record, with perhaps the addition of a Rowing Blue, were strong recommendations. Michael Hillary endeavoured to guide Richard into a proper way of thought, and Richard agreed, reserving the ultimate desire to write. "I shall row myself into the Sudan," he said with youthful arrogance, adding an epigrammatic description: "a country of Blacks ruled by Blues."

This cynical remark won applause among his contemporaries at Shrewsbury, and delighted Oxford youthful society, when he repeated it there. But discipline is as necessary for an oarsman as for success in other Public School activities, as Richard was painfully to discover. To a point he could conform, but at that point at which obedience and subjection must become blind, the point at which no questions must be asked, Richard was inclined to argue; and the system, so much stronger than he, with the force of more than a century since Dr. Arnold's time to propel it, overbore him. "I am going to hate it all," he had reiterated to his mother. And when she had said, "And they are probably going to hate you," the awful possibility that he might not be the centre of the drama had struck him dumb. So now, with everything to recommend him in the eyes of other boys, success at games, a sufficient scholarship, self-reliance, independence, courage, and charm, he affected — as is sometimes the way of the over-gifted among boys — a cynical detachment as to the value of the prizes and awards on which the schoolboy mind sets so much store.

His housemaster, Mr. Whitfield, sums him up in saying :

> He seemed to dislike the conventional views of things, often merely because they were conventional. He would often express views merely because he thought they were contrary to those of his companions, and would seem disappointed if his ideas were accepted without argument.
>
> He hated above all being treated as young, as though he were not a man of the world. He liked shocking people in a mild way. An instance may show the point. A Board of Education Inspector visited the school and lunched at the head table in Richard's house. The Inspector sat on the housemaster's right, and Richard opposite him. Richard leaned across the table and opened the conversation with the remark : " You have come to inspect the masters here, not the boys, haven't you ? " The remark was received by everyone, I fancy, better than he had hoped.

In a different way, I think, than he had expected. Richard had seized the chance of disputing the value of the Public School system with an Inspector of Education, his enjoyment of argument taking added flavour from the expectation of doing this under the immediate eye of his housemaster. Instead, everyone roared as at a joke. The enquirer was silent. The chance had failed him.

His attitude of a man of the world was not entirely unjustified. From his thirteenth birthday he had gone abroad every year by himself. His parents could come home only in the summer. At Easter and at Christmastime the houses of relatives were open to him, or the alternative of remaining at the Whitfields'. But at that early stage he had produced an alternative of his own ; that he should go abroad to France and Germany, live in a *pension*, and improve his languages. The family in Khartoum gave reluctant agreement, and soon got used to it. Each year he travelled by himself, usually to Germany. These were the years when Hitler had come to power. Richard, taking himself off to different *pensions* in Germany during these years, watched with a youthful but cynical eye Hitler's dogma-fed youth preparing for the day that was soon to come. He guessed that in a few years he would be fighting them ; and the prospect he found intensely interesting. It was like invading the training quarters of a rival crew. He learned to speak German, and debated with German youths the mistakenness of their aims. His air of wary cynicism may have been discounted by the Germans ; if not, then he must have seemed to them a living testimony to their assumption that English youth was decadent.

Back at the head table at Mr. Whitfield's house

after holidays such as that, it must have been difficult to hide the pretensions to being a man of the world.

Peter Pease, doing admirably at Eton, was at this time spending his holidays at his parents' home in Yorkshire, shooting during the Christmas holidays, hunting in the spring, growing better-looking every year, more and more appearing the "verray parfit gentil knight" that Richard later found him to be. Richard, the unconventional Richard, was becoming at the same stage "the amazing Mr. Hillary", who, in their short fierce companionship, both worried and fascinated Peter Pease.

★

In 1937 he left Shrewsbury and in October entered Trinity College, Oxford, as an undergraduate. In the freer air of Oxford he was to find the perfect background for his unconventional temperament, and the two years he spent there were to be the happiest of his life.

Oxford was a deeply felt experience for Richard, as it has been for many men. It was to provide the background for his emotional development. It was to give him both his first and last taste of spiritual and intellectual freedom. It was to enrich him with friendships which survived even death. It received him as a charming egocentric, proudly conscious of his privileges, his superiority to others, and softened his hardness with an awareness, an almost painful awareness, of what friendship could mean.

When Richard went up to Oxford in October 1937 he was an unusually good-looking boy of eighteen, with a rowing reputation from his school, with enough wit, self-assurance and connections to guarantee for him entrance to some of the more exclusive clubs, and the friendship of a number of hard-spirited young gentlemen, both in Trinity and other colleges. The pattern was laid out to make life amusing and interesting, if not entirely profitable, for him. Because he came from one of the better public schools, and brought with him a reputation as an oarsman, and because he came unencumbered by scholarship, with no duty to take a good degree, but with every equipment to do so should he feel so inclined, the clique into which he was to fall was waiting for him.

It was one that suited Richard temperamentally. Mr. Whitfield has remarked his desire to be taken as a man of the world. At Trinity in 1937 his tastes could be indulged. Parents, masters, the strict observance of rules, unceasing supervision, which had been the background of life at Shrewsbury, had greatly mitigated against the display of worldly tendencies. At Oxford the barriers to maintaining this attitude did not exist. Supervision was limited, dons did not intrude, the rules were framed for adults, not for children. Suddenly the glory of manhood was upon him.

Richard was quite aware that he was in a privileged position. The undergraduates who come up to Oxford every year do so from nearly every walk of life, and every quarter of the kingdom. There are varieties of colleges and an infinity of distinctions among cliques. Trinity was a small but rich college. Afterwards Richard could not contain the boast that in his time it included the president of the Rugby Club, the secretary of the Boat Club, numerous golf, hockey and running Blues, the best cricketer in the University, the president of the Dramatic Society, and the editor of the *Isis*, the Undergraduate magazine. There was in addition a small but select band of scholars. These last were in a minority, the lesser jewels in the crown of Trinity's glory. Held up to a certain light they glowed, but their effulgence was of a dim quality in comparison with the glory that radiated from the presence and prowess of the athletic members, who set the tone of alert Philistinism that Trinity was pleasantly aware was characteristic of it.

Into this pattern Richard fitted with ease and was made welcome by those already established in it.

It happened that Trinity had for some sixty years languished in the Head of the River races ; though the galaxy of its stars in every branch of sport was numerous, in rowing the College had made no particular mark. Richard was therefore an asset. He was not enough to make a boat crew in himself, but he arrived at a propitious moment when others had come up with rowing experience, to bring Trinity to the fore on the river, as it was in every other sport. As a Freshman he rowed stroke in the Trinity boat and, for the first time since 1865, Trinity came to the head of the river. It held that place until the war ended the official races, and Richard was sufficiently prominent, as the member of the crew who had chiefly contributed to that achievement, to enjoy a special position, both in the College and in the University at large.

It was typical of the alert Philistine that he did not neglect the intellectual side of life. He must be intelligent as well as athletic. Richard joined the staff of the *Isis*, his friendship with the editor, who was a member of his college, giving him the necessary introduction. He became sports editor, and spent much time at this occupation, encouraged, when he thought of his neglected reading, by the notion that he was training himself as a journalist.

Conversation was considered a worthy art — conversation as opposed to debate. The Union was frowned upon, but animated discussion took place in each other's rooms at night. " One could enter anybody's rooms ", he recorded in *The Last Enemy*, " and within two minutes be engaged in a heated discussion over orthodox versus Fairbairn rowing, or whether

Ezra Pound or T. S. Eliot was the daddy of contemporary poetry."

But one subject was not debated: that was the question of liberty. The matter was too personal; besides everyone was uneasily aware that the point was shortly to be put to a grave practical test.

Even thus early, the signs of approaching war were manifest. A University Air Squadron was formed, training was offered free at Government expense, and several afternoons a week undergraduates who would have been embarrassed if their purpose had been construed as preparing themselves to defend their country, went to the flying field, outside Oxford, were exercised in Link trainers, and taught to fly by R.A.F. instructors.

Richard, with most of his friends, joined the University Air Squadron, and regarded with scorn the serious-minded types who had joined the O.T.C. and spent the afternoons in field exercises. War was certainly to come, but the only possible way in which to deal with it was to regard it as a sport. As Richard put it:

> In a fighter plane, I believe, we have found a way to return to war as it ought to be, war which is individual combat between two people, in which one either kills or is killed. It's exciting, it's individual, and it's disinterested. I shan't be sitting behind a long-range gun working out how to kill people sixty miles away. I shan't get maimed:

either I shall get killed or I shall get a few pleasant putty medals and enjoy being stared at in a night club.

That was the attitude — to pretend that the thing was a bore, but that if forced to take part in it one might as well have the best time possible.

His friends were of the same mind. Since nearly all of them were to go with him into the Air Force when, in that Long Vacation of 1939, the war at last broke out, and since they were all to play a part in his story, a few of them, who may stand as examples of the rest, should be introduced now.

There was Frank Waldron, who rowed No. 6 in the Oxford crew, who stood six-foot-three and had an impressive mass of snow-white hair. Frank was popular. The girls pursued him, but Richard records that he affected to prefer drink. Richard describes him as being, except for himself, the laziest oarsman in the University, but says that he was the most stylish. He had Richard's entire devotion. With eight others, Richard and Frank, with designed cunning and a superior manner, visited Germany and Hungary on the eve of war, at the German and Hungarian Governments' expense, having represented themselves, not untruthfully, as an Oxford University crew. They carried off from Germany the Hermann Goering Cup; but in Budapest, where the Danube instead of being blue turned out to be a turbulent brown, and where a rich diet of goulash and Tokay, and an extremely hot day, made them not at their best, they were defeated. But medals were struck in Budapest in their honour, and the Hungarians at a subsequent banquet outdid themselves in eloquence and compliments.

Noel Agazarian was one of the more endearing of the select company at Oxford. His boldness matched Richard's. Noel had an Armenian father and a French mother. He was, in Richard's description, " by nature cosmopolitan, intelligent, and a brilliant linguist, but an English education had discovered that he was an athlete, and his University triumphs had been of brawn rather than brain. Of this he was very well aware and somewhat bewildered by it. These warring elements in his nature made him a most amusing companion and a very good friend."

Noel, sprung from such a parentage, was to die in flames in the Battle of Britain, which indicates that the faithful brotherhood of English school and university is stronger than family ties. Not to die with the brotherhood was unthinkable for this young gentleman who in every gesture and intonation of voice, in the account Richard gives of him, is indistinguishable from the others with whom he had shared school and Oxford. His face had an indefinable charm, without being conventionally good-looking; with his dark countenance and foreign appearance he was as unlike an Englishman as it was possible to be.

Yet the few years of his boyhood in the society of English schools had wiped away, from his outward manner at least, if not from his heart and mind, all traces of foreign birth. On leave from their first flying station in the war, Richard and Noel went over to Skye. Neither was an Englishman, but this adventure and the way in which it is described is characteristically English. Is it training, and not birth then, that makes the pattern that we call English ?

. . . The inn-keeper welcomed us and showed us our rooms. From every window was the same view, grey mountains rising in austere beauty, their peaks hidden in a white mist, and everywhere a great feeling of stillness. The shadows that lengthened across the valley, the streams that coursed down the rocks, the thin mist turning now into night, all a part of that stillness. I shivered. Skye was a world that one would either love or hate ; there could be no temporizing.

" It is very beautiful," said the landlord.

" Yes," I said, " it's beautiful."

" But only mountaineers or fools will climb those peaks."

" We're both fools," Noel said shortly.

" So be it. Dinner is at 8.30."

We stood a while at the window. The night was clear and our heads felt clear and cold as the air. We smelled the odour of the ground in the spring after rain and behind us the wood smoke of the pine fire in our room, and we were content. For these are the odours of nostalgia, spring mist and wood smoke, and never the scent of a woman or of food.

We were alone in the inn save for one old man who had returned there to die. His hair was white but his face and bearing were still those of a mountaineer, though he must have been a great age. He never spoke, but appeared regularly at meals to take his place at a table tight-pressed against the window, alone with his wine and his memories. We thought him rather fine.

In the morning we set off early, warmed by a rare spring sun which soon dried the dew from the heather. We had decided on Bruach-na-Free, one of the easier peaks, but it was lunch-time before we reached the base of the first stiff climb and the muscles in our thighs were already taut. We rested and ate our sandwiches and drank from a mountain stream. The water was achingly cold. Then we started to climb. In the morning we had taken our time and talked, now we moved fast and said nothing. With feet and hands we forced our way up the lower grey crumbling rock to the wet black smooth surface, mist-clouded above. There was no friendship in that climb: neither of us had spoken, but each knew that the other meant to reach the top first. Once I slipped and dropped back several feet, cutting my hand. Noel did not stop; he did not even turn his head. I would not have forgiven him if he had. Gradually I brought him back. Nothing disturbed that great stillness but the occasional crash of a loose stone and the sobbing of our breath. We were no longer going up and around the face of the mountain but climbing straight. We could see nothing in the mist, but my thigh muscles were twitching with the strain and my arms were on fire. Then I felt a cold breeze blowing down on my upturned face and knew we were near the top. I practically threw myself up the last few yards, but Noel hung on to his advantage and hauled himself up the last ledge with a gasp of relief, a second or two before me. We lay on our backs, and felt the black wet rock cold against us, felt the deep mist damp against our faces, felt the sweat as it trickled into our eyes, felt the air in deep gulps within our lungs. The war was far away and life was very good.

We could see nothing below us, but started off down, jumping and slithering on the avalanche of rocks that cascaded beside us, making a great thunder of noise in that deep stillness. We soon felt again the sun, warm on our faces, and saw below us the bed of a mountain stream leading away into the distance, and scarcely visible, a mere speck at the far end, the inn. We did not hesitate to follow the stream, as it was running low, and we made quite good time until we came to a drop of some twelve feet where the water fell in a small torrent. This we managed to negotiate without getting too wet, only to be met a few yards further on with a sheer drop of some twenty feet. The stream had become a river and dropped down into a shallow pool some two feet deep. It was impossible to go back and there was only one way of going on. "You first," I said to Noel. "Give me your clothes and I'll throw them down to you with mine."

Now early in March is no time for bathing anywhere, but there can be few colder places that we could have chosen than the mountain streams of Skye. Noel stripped, handed me his clothes, and let himself down as far as possible. Then he let go. He landed on all fours and scrambled out unhurt, a grotesque white figure amidst those sombre rocks.

"For Christ's sake hurry up : I'm freezing."

"I'm right with you," I shouted, and then with Noel's clothes firmly clutched under my arm, and still wearing my own, I slipped. I had a short glimpse of Noel's agonized face watching the delicate curve of one of his shoes through the air and then I was under the water with two grazed knees. It was freezingly cold, but I managed to grab everything and wallowed painfully out.

" You bastard," said Noel.

" I'm sorry, but look at me : I'm just as wet."

" Yes, but you're wearing your clothes : I've got to put these bloody things on again."

With much muttering he finally got dressed, and we squelched our way onwards. By the time we reached the inn two hours later we were dry but mighty hungry.

Over dinner we told the landlord of our novel descent. His sole comment was " Humph," but the old man at the window turned and smiled at us. I think he approved.

Then there was Peter Howes, *maigre* and with cadaverous good looks, disguising the uncomfortable evidence that he had a brain by constantly talking of everything save that which was nearest to his heart — science. He was never happier, Richard records, than when, " lying back smoking his pipe, he could expound his theories on sex (of which he knew very little), on literature (of which he knew more), and on mathematics (of which he knew a great deal) ".

War had not been part of Peter's calculations. He was reading for a science degree, and trying unobtrusively to do well. Obedient to the bonds of the brotherhood he joined the Oxford University Air Squadron, and with the others was swept into the R.A.F. when hostilities started. Peter Howes, with his permanently harassed expression, hitherto devoted to searching out the mysteries of science, now turned to concentrate on the unknown of aeronautics. The brotherhood gave to the R.A.F. the same ironic, detached interest they had offered to Oxford. Peter was to the faith faithful, but he could not preserve the necessary detachment. Aeronautics, though not pure science, was related. From an almost morbid introspection, an unhappy preoccupation with the labyrinths of his own mind, his personality in the world of the R.A.F. blossomed, like some plant long untouched by the sun, into an at first unwilling but soon eager acceptance of the ideas and habits of others. In three months, reports Richard, he was an excellent pilot and his vocabulary was pure R.A.F. But his allegiance to a new and larger brotherhood was to be of short duration. He had a term of aching anxiety during the early part of the Battle of Britain because he had not shot anyone down. Then he met his end bravely, fighting over Hornchurch, and the young gentleman who, only a little more than a year before, had been animadverting loquaciously to his young contemporaries on life and literature, and had abandoned learning for the R.A.F., adopting the phlegmatic attitude and brief slang that were its characteristics, now abandoned life too.

★

Oxford was a period of quickening activity in every way. Life assumed adult proportions. Every privilege of manhood was suddenly open, including that of falling in love. But there was inevitably a powerful sense of frustration in this. One couldn't marry, being penurious, and seduction is never as easy as it is popularly supposed to be. This is especially the case when the object of one's ardour is young and lovely, and not as carefree with her reputation as an athletic young Philistine can afford to be. Richard was driven nearly mad by frustration, and since love cannot support an endless debate, nor withstand having each carefully-laid plot shiver into nothing against the hard obduracy of a careful virtue, the thing died. But not before its little thread had become a part of a larger tapestry. The Battle of Britain broke when Richard's first love affair was dying of inanition. Richard had ceased to be an undergraduate and had become a pilot. His life had become linked with that of Peter Pease, and his volatile mind had suddenly sobered. He considered proposing marriage to Anne, but before anything could happen he was shot down. She tried to see him in hospital, but it was impossible at the time. And when he had recovered sufficiently to see visitors, Peter's Denise had entered his life. Richard, scarred by battle, was a very different Richard from the self-centred young undergraduate who first met Anne in 1938, when Trinity had triumphed at the Head of the

River, and Richard Hillary had been the glass of fashion for the fashionably tough and worldly young undergraduate of that time.

So much both of what Richard was in himself and of what his set was like is apparent in the letters that he wrote to Anne that the inclination to quote from them is irresistible. He was in his nineteenth year. The letters he later wrote to Mary from Charter Hall just before his death were written when he was twenty-three. The contrast is remarkable. The letters to Mary are written by a man whose love has been fulfilled ; those to Anne are by a youth in the first frenzy of youthful passion. The writer of the earlier letters is charmingly concerned only with himself ; in the later letters his view is larger, and embraces, with wonderful sympathy and understanding, everyone at his Station. In the letters to Anne, the boy Richard who had sailed successfully through his young life, had charmed everybody, had been liked for his looks and admired for his wit, aims at this new prize with characteristic and winning directness. In the last letters, he is humbled, he has " learnt a little wisdom and a little patience ".

But it is with the bright young undergraduate that we are concerned at the moment, suddenly caught by a vision most charming and feminine at a University party. The alert young Philistine of Trinity College loses no time in getting at essentials.

April 22nd, 1939

Why haven't you got a telephone number — or if you have, am I allowed to know what it is? I feel sure the dance will be dull, and I shall have no compunction about leaving it early. Can you come out later in the evening? There is a friend of mine from Trinity going along, and he and his partner can make up a foursome. Do say you will come. I would suggest another night, but I cannot get permission off during training for Eights week more than once in a blue moon. We galley-slaves are wedded to our oars and only a temporary disaffection is allowed.

Our Commem Ball is on June 20th, so don't cross the Atlantic before then, will you?

Do send me your telephone number as I hate writing letters — even to you. (That, I suppose, you label technique — but I can't cure myself all at once.)

Oxford now in the sunshine is quite delightful — largely because I have had no work to do, and spend most afternoons flying. I suppose you are being the social butterfly and flitting from one dance to the next. Don't become too old and bored before I see you again, and don't forget of London night life that

" *plus ça change, plus c'est la même chose.*"

I must stop before I start writing you a treatise on my favourite topic.

Love,

RICHARD HILLARY.

And again, a little later. The " galley-slave wedded to his oar " looks forward to being distracted :

11*th May*, 1939

Are you coming up here for Eights? They begin a week today and continue till the following Wednesday.

Above HEAD OF THE RIVER

GOING INTO ACTION *Below*

If we stay Head of the River we are giving a cocktail party on our barge on the last night, to which you must come.

I must see you again soon, but I'm quite broke so I can't come to London yet awhile.

I'm feeling very tired — too much rowing and too little work and I look forward to having you brighten me up a bit.

Love,

DICK.

Ten days later, a symptom of love is declared. He has been composing poetry. But the background is activity on the river. Here is the Philistine at his most alert, one who can turn out a sonnet in between stiff training with the oars :

21*st May*, 1939

I do hope you're coming up on Wednesday — even if we don't have a cocktail party. This may not be possible with a Bump Supper following at 8.30 P.M. Please come as I'm longing to see you again.

Yesterday was amusing — as there were crowds of people — it was quite fine, and we managed to stay Head more easily than had been expected.

I miss my career in the air, but not as much as I miss you.

I object to being called matter-of-fact, and I guarantee to beat you in any " whimsy " contest you like to organize.

The spring has had a bad effect on me and I have burst into verse — also composed a song about mountains and the moons and you ! You must hear it sometime. It will thaw the icy walls of your heart.

RICHARD.

But it is difficult to maintain the superior man-of-the-world attitude for long. Poor Richard's heart was becoming involved. Anne could write letters too, and with feminine guile could prick the little bubbles of his conceits. Richard was wordy in defending his point of view, but Anne was worth conceding a few points of principle.

26th June, 1939

I have been meaning to write to you ever since going to Henley, but this is the first quiet moment that I have had. As you see, I'm at home for tonight and rather bored. Yesterday we rowed at Marlow Regatta in our four to tune up for Henley. If we were to win we had to row five times in one day. By the end of the fourth race I was so tired I could not see and cursed the day that made me go to a Commem. However we did have to race again and Sammy steered us into the bank when we had the race in our pocket. However, now at any rate I am beginning to feel fit again.

I did love having you up on Wednesday. I only hope you enjoyed coming ? As you see my brain is completely addled. I shall start writing about the weather in a minute instead of about the things that I really want to say to you.

You left your handkerchief in the car. It has lost its scent and looks a little crumpled — rather like you on Thursday morning, — but it reminds me of you and that there are other things in life besides rowing men who bicker all day and silly little boats that must be propelled up and down the river.

Please write to me soon. As soon as you vanish from my sight now I imagine that I have done something awful and that I shall receive a fearsome note asking what I meant by so and so or such and such. In fact you have as much grip over me as a wife which *won't do at all.* I must escape from the shackles and I don't have to be near you to hear you say that you aren't making it very difficult.

RICHARD.

Anne disappears to France, and Richard writes from the depths of a great depression :

16th July, 1939

Last night I decided that I could not possibly stay at home so I went out with a couple of men from Cambridge. It was the worst thing I could have done as we went to a fair and the awful roundabout ground out " Deep Purple " all night. So I came home only to hear " wishing will make it so " being played on the wireless. That was too much and I just gave up and went to bed. I'm afraid it's going to be a case of

" Music when soft voices die
Vibrates in the memory."

Was it a good ball last night ? I spend all my time thinking of you, and trying to imagine what you're thinking and how you're looking. But it is very difficult and I cannot see you clearly at all. You're almost there all the time but it's rather like an awful nightmare. I can almost reach you but not quite, as there is a thick veil in between just blurring you. I wish I had a photograph and then at least I'd have a permanent image of you. All sorts of unpleasant people whom I don't want to think about at all keep popping into my mind with fearful clarity but they won't go away and let you in instead.

I hope you're going to be happy and forget, if that is

what you want to do — because there is no good in us both moping around on opposite sides of the channel.

Sometimes now I wish there would be a war — as I feel then that so many things would clarify themselves and you and I could be together again anyhow for a short time and there would be no false values and muddled thinking. Life would have a purpose while it lasted. I'm afraid that I'm becoming very heavy and rather boring. But a young man in love was ever a pitiable object. I wish I could be with you now — have you in my arms, but the day when I shall be able to do that again seems very remote.

RICHARD.

The letters go on until April 1940, when Richard is in Morayshire at his Flying Training School. They go on to the point where the story in *The Last Enemy* begins ; to that moment when Hitler invaded Denmark, and the Germans began to overrun Europe. Young men did not all automatically fall out of love at that time, but the shock was sharp enough to distract Richard's mind from an affair that had been too much protracted without satisfaction of any kind. Some hint of the folly of his pursuit impressed him, too, now that he had fallen into the habit of measuring himself against the stillness and serenity of Peter Pease.

★

There is something most moving in every account and glimpse that is given of these Oxford years in Richard's letters. Generations come, and pass away, but a particular sadness seems in retrospect to attach to those whom we see afterwards to have been poised on the edge of doom. Dining in their high halls, active in their narrow boats, talking in their quiet rooms, or flying with instructors on their spare afternoons ; every glimpse that is caught of them is of a fierce mental and physical activity ; and suddenly comes a deathly silence, and they are gone.

In July 1939 Richard went with the Oxford University Air Squadron to Lympne for a course of training. Anne was in France, and he, who had not yet flown solo, was already meditating the possibility of borrowing a plane and flying over to see her. But he was stopped by the chastening thought that no plane was allowed outside the three-mile limit, and " if I crashed in France I should get kicked out of the Reserve, straight into the militia for six months — which obviously wouldn't do at all ".

" Actually," he says airily, " I haven't been doing any solo flying lately as when I had my solo test with the Squadron Leader he started yelling and shouting down the speaking tube, so I disconnected him, thinking he was a thoroughly bad thing for the nerves. I could see him gesticulating wildly in front, and when I landed I gathered that he was trying to get me to do right-hand turns. He failed entirely to take the big view, and a tentative suggestion on my part that it was rather funny did not seem to have the hilarious effect that I had hoped for, and I now fly under strong supervision. Were it possible to crowd two instructors into the plane he would do it. However, là, là and vum ! vum ! it cannot be helped ! "

But in spite of this he got in the requisite number of hours solo flying for his A licence. Moments of suspense dampened his ebullience even then.

> On Friday I scared myself out of my wits. I was supposed to be practising climbing turns on my own when I got into a spiral dive. I came tearing through the clouds to find the earth looming up at a most alarming rate so I counted my buttons and muttered a prayer to the Only person who means anything to me and who I thought might hear me and sure enough the 'plane flattened out at 100 feet and glided like a bird.

*

Richard, with his father and mother, then went to France on a motoring holiday. As the war drew near, and it was plain that it could not be avoided, they headed for Boulogne and arrived in England only three days before the fateful Sunday. Beaconsfield is not far from Oxford, and on that Sunday morning, September 3rd, when the Prime Minister had ceased speaking on the wireless, Richard took his father's car, said goodbye to his parents, and drove over to Oxford to report to the Headquarters of the University Air Squadron.

There, throughout the day, his friends collected.

War was here at last and it was impossible any longer to treat training as a comic diversion from other sports. Richard was made a sergeant, issued with a uniform and put in charge of a platoon. He wore the three stripes as a sign of his authority, but he could not discard immediately the air of a Philistine, though this was inappropriate in the commander of a platoon. But the members of his platoon being his fellow undergraduates, compromise was possible when no superior officer was about. Some form of compromise was inevitable because Richard, like most of the other platoon commanders, had taken his training so lightly that he did not know the proper words of command or on what foot of his marching platoon to issue them. The platoon, on being consulted, agreed that the democratic principle should be respected, seeing that that was what the war was being fought about. It was therefore agreed with Sergeant Hillary that a majority show of hands should determine what was the next move the platoon should make, and for two weeks drill was carried out in this way.

Then Richard was given a commission and moved with others to an Initial Training Wing. This delighted him, for it meant that at last he could get away from the parade ground and up in an aeroplane. Here he found Frank Waldron, Noel Agazarian and Michael Judd, Nigel Bicknell, Bill Aitken and Dick

Holdsworth. But again flying was postponed. Instead they found themselves on a pier jutting out from a south-coast town, where, under the command of regular Air Force drill sergeants, they were mercilessly drilled for several hours a day. At the end of a fortnight of this they received their postings for flying training schools and Richard, with several of his contemporaries, was instructed to report to a small village on the north-east coast of Scotland.

Here, under Sergeant White, Richard really learnt to fly. Sergeant White had had many trainees through his hands and his method was no doubt similar in every case.

> For weeks [reported Richard] he sat behind me in the rear cockpit muttering, just loud enough for me to hear, about the bad luck of getting such a bum for a pupil. Then one day he called down the Inter-Comm., "Man, you can fly at last. Now I want you to dust the pants of Agazarian and show our friend, Sergeant Robinson [Agazarian's instructor], that he's not the only one with a pupil that's not a half-wit."

One of the most entrancing chapters in *The Last Enemy* is the description of life in this flying school in north-east Scotland. The war had not yet come near them, and the friends of Trinity had merely transferred their debates and fun from their rooms overlooking the Quads at Oxford to a little village by the North Sea. They had time for relaxation, they went on holidays together to Skye, or shooting on the Duke of Hamilton's estate. The war across the water in France was static and they had a feeling of desperation that they would never see a bullet fired or come anywhere near the enemy. It was like going out all day with a gun and never flushing a partridge. A certain irritability developed between them, which was really due to a sense of frustration and a shamed feeling that, having departed as heroes to train for this combat, they would shortly be returning as undergraduates to put their noses into books again.

Then the course finished, and they had to move on. They had taken their Wings Examination, and were now fully fledged Pilot Officers. They awaited their postings with impatience. These, when they came, were a shock. Only two out of the whole course were to go into fighters, for at this stage of the war there had been very few casualties in Fighter Command. Richard, Noel and Peter Howes were assigned to Army Co-operation, which meant a further course of training at Old Sarum before they could become operational ; and, oh, the shame of it, operational in Lysanders, " flying coffins ", in Peter Howes' gloomy phrase. So much for the bright dreams of knightly combat in the air which had been the vision they had entertained at Oxford. Noel, Peter and Richard drove down to Old Sarum together in a state of some depression.

Here, amongst the Lysanders and the Hectors, Richard, Noel and Peter found a few old friends, and Richard found two companions, Peter Pease and Colin Pinckney, who had been together since the beginning of the war and were now inseparable. Peter and Colin had been at Cambridge together and had both been in the Cambridge University Air Squadron. Richard, Peter and Colin were drawn to one another, and together they formed a triangle of friendship which is the theme of *The Last Enemy*.

★

Then, with terrible suddenness, Dunkirk was in the news and reinforcements were needed for the fully trained Fighter squadrons who were covering the evacuation from the beaches. Suddenly the sport was over, there was no room for anything but seriousness, the bitter game for which these tranquil months had been a preparation had now to be played. The newspapers were headlined with the appeals of the Government urging people not to evacuate, and in the training squadron they were called to parade while the chief instructor rose to his feet and told them, without decorating the thing, of the squadrons they would now have to make up, and the seriousness of the moment.

Richard, with fifteen of his friends including Bill Aitken and Peter Pease, was sent to a training unit in Gloucestershire for a fortnight to complete his training before being drafted to a Fighter squadron. At the end of the course he walked down to the Adjutant's office with Peter Pease and Colin Pinckney, and found that 603 (City of Edinburgh) Squadron had three vacancies, and the three of them could go together.

★

On the surface, in manner and upbringing, Peter and Colin were indistinguishable from Richard, Noel Agazarian, Peter Howes and Frank Waldron. But in Peter Pease there was a subtle difference, distinctly apparent to the enquiring eye and the profound and ceaseless questioner that Richard had remained from boyhood. Peter, he saw, was the ultimate perfection of the pattern into which he and the others had consciously fitted themselves — that of young men of the world of the better-off classes. It was to this end that their education had been devised. But Richard had always had an instinctive revulsion against all doctrines and orthodoxy which presented themselves in the form of a Faith or a System. He had been happy enough in his membership of the caste. These were his friends, he spoke with their accent, and thought as they did ; on them all his affections and thoughts were centred. Suddenly, finding in Peter the ultimate perfection which the system could devise, all that he had accepted unthinkingly seemed to him to demand explanation. What made them all like this? To what end was such an expensively-fashioned nobility designed? He had occasionally, and for the sake of the laughter it had evoked, laid light ridicule on the System at Shrewsbury and Trinity. The instinct to question it had been there all the time, but it had been left unanswered in the carefree, onward surge of life. But now, seeing in Peter Pease the perfection of the System, he could not remove from him his fascinated gaze, or let him alone, but must be for ever questioning him, trying to plumb his motives and what he wanted of life. And cheated at last of the truth because Peter was killed, he turned to Denise, Peter's fiancée; and all the course of his young life, through him and through her, and through the awakening of his sleeping spirit for which they were responsible, was altered by the fact that Peter Pease and Colin Pinckney, and the girl Peter was to marry, Denise, came upon this detached and self-sufficient young man in the months just before he was to play his brief and exciting part in the Battle of Britain.

★

Richard, at this stage, took a coolly objective view of life. His good looks, the charm of his personality, and his position in Oxford undergraduate society, combined to intensify his rather hardy self-assurance. His capacity for mischief, which had grown with him since boyhood, got him into many scrapes, from the majority of which he was able to extricate himself by a combination of insolence and charm in the d'Artagnan manner. Success in such enterprises, particularly when confounding authority, had won him the esteem of the brotherhood. The touch of arrogance in his character was fortified by this. When he went into the R.A.F. he did not change this attitude. He was prepared to treat the service as he had treated the University, as bumbling authority not to be taken too seriously. As for the war, well, it offered some chances of excitement and happily postponed the necessity of taking up his career.

He might have continued to regard the whole enterprise with sardonic derision had it not been for Peter Pease. Richard continued to behave arrogantly — the habit was too long-seated to be discarded easily — but every time he had a talk with Peter his ebullience subsided, and he began to question himself. Then he began to question Peter, trying, as he had done when small, to get at the truth behind the quiet reserve that masked Peter's true feelings. He began by admiring Peter, he went on to envy him, and he ended by loving him.

Colin Pinckney, who was to form the third corner of the triangle of friendship recorded in *The Last Enemy*, was more forthcoming than Peter. Peter and Colin had been friends for a very long time, each supplemented the other, and the understanding between them was complete. Colin was a sportsman. To him the chief pleasures in life were to be derived from a grouse-shoot and a salmon river. He and Peter had no need to question each other ; they took the same values for granted, and the bonds holding them to one another had no need to be defined. The strange, erratic, unpredictable young man who suddenly occupied their attention they accepted in their calm, reserved way. They must sometimes have felt a little flustered by Richard's more sensational exploits, sometimes a little disconcerted by his naïve attempts to search out their motives, which it would never have occurred to them to question. There is evidence that they sometimes felt a little proud of him.

" Our Mr. Hillary," reported Peter to Denise one evening on the telephone, " has just crash-landed in a cabbage-field fifteen miles from here, and has reported to the Station commander that he will return by train when he has attended a cocktail party he found in progress at the first house he reached."

" Our Mr. Hillary " became a legend with Peter and Colin. Reports of his misdemeanours and adventures became commonplace in their letters, but they never tried to rival him in these exploits. They were so sure of themselves in a way that Richard was not ; whose attempts to hide that fact were explicit often in these adventures.

Throughout the first period of their training at

Old Sarum the three of them had become inseparable. The time was just before Dunkirk. The war seemed a remote thing, like an examination for which one would eventually have to sit ; a threat, not a present danger. To Richard, it was still as though he were at Trinity ; to Colin, it meant enforced abstinence from the mayfly ; to Peter, I think, it was a period of quiet reflection, or so quiet as Mr. Hillary would allow, before a giant grappling. They had worked together in their course, and they spent the hours off duty together. I have a glimpse of the three of them, all over six-feet-two, elegant in their new uniforms, walking together and engaged in serious conversation. Peter Pease stands out — " the best-looking man I ever knew " — in Richard's quick phrase ; beside him Colin Pinckney, big-framed with bony, attractively ugly face ; and with them Richard, zestful, argumentative, bursting with vitality. Peter and Colin smile tolerantly, even with a hint of pride, at the outrageousness of " Mr. Hillary ". Fresh and young, examples of the best that English blood and training can do, they may be glimpsed there, caught in the sunshine, before the storm breaks and they are lost in it.

Chapter Three

PETER and Richard decided to drive up to Edinburgh together to join the Squadron in Peter's car, and to stop overnight at Peter's home in Yorkshire on the way. Colin Pinckney was to drive his own car up, and join them at the Peases' ; then they were to motor on together to Edinburgh.

Richard has recorded that he felt dispirited on that drive. They were going North to join a squadron, when the battle was about to break in the South, and they were motoring through the most depressing part of industrial England. These two things together weighed down his ebullient spirits and gave him a fine opportunity to impress Peter with his experience as a man of the world. "I can go south to France, Italy, or where you will and feel perfectly at home ; but north of Oxford I'm in a foreign country."

Peter did not rise to the bait. Richard no doubt anticipated a warm discussion in which Peter would have defended his native part of England, while he would chant the joys of the warm South. But Peter only remarked quietly : "The people who live in this ugly part of the world will fight this war to the

RICHARD BEFORE THE BATTLE OF BRITAIN

end rather than surrender one inch of it" ; and had steered the conversation politely away from the argument his friend so obviously wanted.

Richard was not really depressed. His gloomy observations about turning their backs on the fighting and on the repellent features of the countryside were intended to draw Peter out. On other scores he had reason to feel satisfied. At least he was going to a Fighter Squadron, and in the company of two men who gave him the greatest satisfaction as friends ; Peter was to do all the driving on this journey ; and Richard confidently anticipated the opportunity of getting behind the quiet reserve with which Peter had so far parried all questions about his attitude to life. Peter had grown fond of Richard, but he found himself sometimes disconcerted by his friend's probing enquiries. Of his own values he was absolutely certain : he was aware that these were not held by everybody. That did not shake his confidence in his own beliefs, nor did his serene and well-ordered mind suffer any feeling of offence because others did not share his views.

Something about Richard touched a chord of sympathy in Peter. His quiet discerning eye saw that Richard was not nearly so sure of himself as his debonair and all-conquering attitude was meant to convey. Peter had never had need to consider his own attitude to life. He accepted happily the destiny which circumstances had drawn for him: the deep affection of his parents and brothers and sister, the attractive home, the happiness of his years at Eton and Cambridge, and the responsibility that he knew would one day be his.

Richard had proved to be one more source of pleasure in his life. He knew that Richard liked him, and he himself felt strangely drawn in turn to this ardent youth who radiated charm, mischief and brilliance, and was always exciting to be with.

It amused him that Richard should always be trying to shock him. Nothing shocks, if you have the right armour. When Richard set out to prove that atheism was the philosophy of the intelligent man, Peter was not outraged: God to this young man, firm in his faith, was real, and he suspected that He was to Richard too, in spite of Richard's emphatic denials. Richard's assertions that he was fighting this war only for what he could get out of it, Peter turned aside with his gentle smile of disbelief; and showed no embarrassment when Richard fiercely asked him to state his own aims in the war. Peter saw no reason to mock the virtues of love of your fellow-men, and the debt one's body owed to England for giving it birth. He never became excited in an argument; tall, handsome, immaculate in his uniform, he could smile across at his flushed, dynamic friend and assert his faith with no fear of appearing ridiculous.

Peter's love for Richard grew after each of these encounters. A spring of tenderness in him welled up and sought to protect Richard from the harshness of life against which he so continually bruised himself. When Richard scoffed at the Public School system, Peter only smiled ; he did no more than say that the happiest of all his years of life had been at Eton. When Richard said fiercely, " In an age when to love one's country is vulgar, to love God archaic, and to love mankind sentimental, you do all three," Peter did not grow angry at the taunt. He merely mildly said, " Something bigger than you or me is coming out of this, Richard, and as it grows you'll grow with it."

What attracted him to Richard was his conviction that beneath the proclaimed disorder of his life was an enormous potentiality for good ; what touched the spring of his tenderness was his realization that Richard was whistling in the dark ; what encouraged him was the certainty that at the right moment Richard would discard his verbal virtuosity for noble and disinterested action.

Colin arrived at the Peases' half an hour after they did. In the dining-room of Peter's lovely home they sat down to dinner. Richard for once was subdued. He said little, but his mind registered much. Something that might mark the end of everything he saw that night hung like a doom in the air, but was ignored.

Yet not ignored, for they spoke of the war, but accepted it without question, or fear, or uncertainty, as the price which one gladly pays to preserve one's birthright. Richard, who had scoffed at Peter's war aims, and had proclaimed that he himself was fighting only for what he could get out of it, fell silent, and records that he felt a new emotion. "It occurred to me that if Peter were killed it would be important — not only to his family, but indeed for me, as the deaths of the majority of my friends, many of whom I knew better, could not be. I was confused and disturbed by this."

This was the first time he had paused in his headlong rush through life to consider the permanent values on which it might be based. At a time when it was the mode to be cynical he had had the equipment to be ultra-cynical: a ready tongue, yet a charm of character which removed the sharp edges of his wit and made it attractive. His success at Oxford had been this kind of success; life to him had been a joy flashing past; an endless frieze of joy whose onward movement had never so far ceased. And abruptly for this moment it did cease, and so many of the figures in the frieze, and those in particular whom he had most admired, were caught in the fantastic and unreal nature of their gestures; while a few that had seemed the comic element among the others were seen in fact to be noble and sincere. It was a shock to the scoffer.

For the first time he failed to find a ready retort. " I was confused and disturbed by this."

But why was he " confused and disturbed " ? Was it because he saw suddenly how cheap were wit and cynicism in face of those virtues of faith and honest purpose which Peter exemplified in his life, and which he now saw were not hypocritically assumed ? Or because a tide of feeling was rising in him for Peter, a tide so rapid and strong that at this moment it engulfed the cynical response which was his automatic reaction to any show of emotion ?

I do not think that at that time Richard knew what was the reason for his sudden attraction to Peter. Far more than the drawing-power of comradeship in the Squadron, admiration for his looks, or mere curiosity to discover the explanation of such unusual serenity of mind, attracted him. Richard continually sought for the explanation.

> I resented this [Peter's] assurance, basically because here was a man better orientated than I, and as the result of an upbringing and a system of education which I deeply distrusted and had in the past despised as being quite incapable of producing anything but, at the best, congenital idiots, and at the worst, fox-hunting bounders. For he was a product of the old-school-tie system in its most extreme form. He was more than comfortably off ; his father owned property which in due course, as the eldest son, he would inherit ; he had been brought up in the orthodox Tory tradition and in the belief that this was as it should be.

And again :

> I resented Peter's self-confidence, for while he was shy, he was perfectly assured. I rather prided myself on my self-sufficiency, on my ability to be perfectly at ease with people of any standing or any age, but with Peter I felt, as it were, that at any moment he might discover me wearing a made-up tie. He would, of course, not be so tactless as to mention it, would in fact put himself out to be even more charming than before. But there it would be. . . . Well, damn it, why shouldn't I wear a made-up tie if I wanted to ?

But while he resented Peter's assurance and self-confidence because they seemed to reflect badly on his own, there was another reason for this increasing absorption of his thoughts with Peter. Richard was suffering a change in his own outlook ; he was sickening, as it were, for a drastic alteration of purpose. His instinct told him — he was more than ordinarily susceptible to the promptings of instinct, as we shall see towards the end of his life — that he had been following the wrong path and must now change direction. He resented this persisting influence, and fought against it ; fought with his reason against it, as Arthur Koestler shows in his discerning essay on Richard ; [1] and seeing in Peter the magnet which drew him towards that change, he became sarcastic and aggressive with him, but could not leave him alone. The account given in *The Last Enemy* of the discussion the two had in the train going from Mon-

1 " The Birth of a Myth ", *Horizon*, April 1943.

trose to Edinburgh is the concentration of arguments which lasted over many months.

The time when they reached Montrose was towards the beginning of August 1940. The battle in the South was intensifying, and Oxford and the past seemed to Richard to be a half-forgotten dream. His love affair with Anne had finally died in April of this year. Something of his youth had gone with Oxford and with her ; so much so that in his last letter to Anne he has to say : "I resent Frank [Waldron] writing in consternation at hearing that I've become a keen aviator. God knows where he heard it." Six months before he would have ridiculed at length the charge of showing keenness about anything, but now the denial is weak, and he does not pursue the subject.

Peter has captured him ; he is beginning to model his conduct on the splendid pattern of Peter's life and thought. He does not forswear the old manner ; on the surface he is still scornful of high ideals, and jests at the expression of serious purpose. He never ceases his attempts to persuade Peter into one false statement that will reveal a flaw of hypocrisy in his attitude ; and he never succeeds. Through all these encounters his love for him grows. When they move South at the end of the month, and into battle, he is fortified by the feeling that Peter is beside him.

He discovers that Peter is in love. Was he jealous of Denise ? In a way I think he was. He did not want to share Peter with anyone. He did not meet Denise, although he knew that she was only a few miles away when they were stationed at Hornchurch. It impressed him that this unknown girl should be on an ack-ack site right in the fighting area. It was like Peter to have that sort of girl.

And although Denise had not met Richard, he was a familiar character to her from Peter and Colin's stories. She formed a picture of someone very gay, high-spirited, scornful of authority ; and because Peter and Colin liked him so much, of someone eminently likeable.

Daily from here she watched the little Spitfires whirling like wounded butterflies to the ground, and did not know, until she was reassured by the sound of his voice on the telephone, or the sight of him descending from his car at the ack-ack site, that Peter had not been in one of these. On one Saturday evening she had seen a plane, with smoke pouring from it, crash-land into a field, and a moment later a parachute, with a figure at the end, swaying slowly to the ground. Peter had telephoned later to say " that was Mr. Hillary ". Colin Pinckney had had his plane shot away in the same fight, and it was Colin who was on the parachute ; a little burned about the hands and mouth but quite cheerful and likely to be in hospital only a short time.

The plane that had crash-landed had been piloted

by Mr. Hillary. No, he wasn't hurt at all. On the contrary : he had rung up to say that he had landed practically in the back garden of a house where a party was in progress, and he would be returning shortly.

It was a time of tightened nerves for them both, but Denise was as like Peter in character as she was afterwards thought by Richard to be in appearance. Of the daily casualty lists they said nothing. Instead Peter talked to her of his friends, giving always a particular account of the exploits of " the amazing Mr. Hillary ", as he often called him.

Then on the night of September 3rd he telephoned Denise. He did not say much, but at the end of a two-minute conversation said " Richard is missing ". Knowing what Richard had meant to Peter, Denise tried to express sympathy, but there was little that could be said. Daily the total of missing and killed was mounting, as the battle intensified. There was less and less opportunity to see Peter, but they exchanged letters when visits or telephone calls were made impossible by the continuing activity.

On Saturday morning, September 14th, Denise had a letter from Peter, saying that Richard had been traced, and was lying badly burned in a hospital, and that he was going to try to go and see him next day.

But on the next day, Sunday, September 15th, at the crisis of the battle, Peter Pease's plane was shot down over Kent and he was instantly killed.

Chapter Four

ON September 3rd, Richard's mother Edwyna Hillary had been on her way down to the Red Cross, where she worked daily, when a terrible feeling of premonition had seized her. At first she thought that she was ill, but then the certainty that something had happened to Richard grew and pressed about her heart. Her husband and Richard had often laughed at her fancies, but this was not to be denied. The morning battle had already started, and had been continuing for some hours, for it was near noon. She knew that Richard must have been somewhere in the sky during that morning, and now she was sure that his plane had been shot down. She bent forward, tapped on the window, and told the driver to take her back to her flat.

But when, shaken with the emotional storm she was passing through, she had let herself into the flat, the rooms were silent and undisturbed. No telephone rang. No telegram lay on the mat. She waited, uneasy, restless and unhappy, by herself in the flat all day; and then towards evening the telephone started its pulsating ring, and with a feeling of impending disaster about to break, she went to answer it. It was Squadron-Leader J. E. A. Fraser, the Station Adjutant, asking for Michael. Too often in these days did Squadron-Leader Fraser have the unhappy task of breaking such news ; it was hard enough with fathers, but to find oneself talking to the mother tried him to the soul. In an endeavour to break the news gently, he wrapped it up into such a glamorized account of Richard's activities, and such a hearty description of how much he was loved in the Squadron, that Edwyna Hillary was forced to break in. She asked him where Richard was. Squadron-Leader Fraser, brought to the point, could only say that he was missing. He had been seen going down in flames over the North Sea that day. But she was not to fear the worst. Boats were out patrolling at all hours, and many survivors had been brought back every day. He hoped to ring her again soon with good news.

When he rang again, it was three hours later. Richard had indeed been rescued, but he was badly burnt. He had been brought to the hospital at Margate, where he had been taken by the boat crew. In a calmer voice than Squadron-Leader Fraser's, Mrs. Hillary asked for explicit directions how to get there. It was almost as difficult to go to Margate at that time as it had been to get to the front-line trenches in the first war, but the next morning she and Michael Hillary went down there.

Nothing of their son was recognizable in the figure with legs and arms heavily bandaged, held up in slings off the bed, and his body slung loosely on straps just clear of the bed ; what remained of his face was completely hidden under a mask of tannic acid, with which burns were treated at that stage. Over this there was a covering of white gauze, which was intended to hide the repellent appearance of the tannic acid mask, but had the effect of making Richard look like a deformed corpse with a light covering over the head. The room in which he lay was in darkness, but he knew that it was his mother by him, for though he drifted in and out of consciousness, he was fully aware in his lucid moments of what went on around him.

He was in this hospital for four days ; it was only a clearing-station, and he had to be moved on as quickly as possible. An ambulance driven and attended by two nervous A.T.S. women came to take him to the Royal Masonic Hospital in London. No flags are flying, no bands playing as the hero moves off in this company, and the voice of Oxford has not been totally dimmed by immersion for several hours in the North Sea, and some almost fatal second-degree burns. Richard is scarred but still dauntless in derision.

. . . with my nurse in attendance, and wrapped in an old grandmother's shawl, I was carried aboard and we were off. For the first few miles I felt quite well, dictated letters to my nurse, drank bottle after bottle of ginger beer, and gossiped with the drivers. They described the countryside for me, told me they were new to the job, expressed satisfaction at having me for a consignment, asked me if I felt fine. Yes, I said, I felt fine ; asked my nurse if the drivers were pretty, heard her answer yes, heard them simpering, and we were all very matey. But after about half an hour my arms began to throb from the rhythmical jolting of the road. I stopped dictating, drank no more ginger beer, and didn't care whether they were pretty or not. Then they lost their way. Wasn't it awful and shouldn't they stop and ask ? No, they certainly shouldn't : they could call out the names of the streets and I would tell them where to go. By the time we arrived at Ravenscourt Park I was pretty much all-in. I was carried into the hospital and once again felt the warm September sun burning my face. I was put in a private ward and had the impression of a hundred excited ants buzzing around me. My nurse said good-bye and started to sob. For no earthly reason I found myself in tears. It had been a lousy hospital, I had never seen the nurse anyway, and I was now in very good hands ; but I suppose I was in a fairly exhausted state. So there we all were, snivelling about the place and getting nowhere. Then the charge nurse came up and took my arm and asked me what my name was.

" Dick," I said.

" Ah," she said brightly. " We must call you Richard the Lion Heart."

I made an attempt at a polite laugh but all that came out was a dismal groan and I fainted away. The house surgeon took the opportunity to give me an anaesthetic and removed all the tannic acid from my left hand.

He was under the anaesthetic for about fifteen minutes, and during that time he saw Peter Pease killed.

He was after another machine, a tall figure leaning slightly forward with a smile at the corner of his mouth. Suddenly from nowhere a Messerschmitt was on his tail about 150 yards away. For two seconds nothing happened. I had a terrible feeling of futility. Then at the top of my voice I shouted, " Peter, for God's sake look out behind ! "

I saw the Messerschmitt open up and a burst of fire hit Peter's machine. His expression did not change, and for a moment his machine hung motionless. Then it turned slowly on its back and dived to the ground. I came-to, screaming his name, with two nurses and the doctor holding me down on the bed.

" All right now. Take it easy, you're not dead yet. That must have been a very bad dream."

I said nothing. There wasn't anything to say. Two days later I had a letter from Colin. My nurse read it to me. It was very short, hoping that I was getting better and telling me that Peter was dead.

*

He spent the next three months at the Royal Masonic Hospital. He was visited by other members of the Squadron, and his mother came and sat with him every day. And here, a fortnight after his arrival, came a visitor whom he did not expect. It was Denise, and he was shocked into a most uncharacteristic silence.

Peter had told him that Denise was beautiful, but he had not expected beauty like this ; and afterwards, when he attempted to describe it in his diary, words failed him. All that he could write was : " She was the most beautiful person I have ever seen ".

After their first shy meeting, she came again and again. She had said the first time : " I hope you'll excuse me coming to see you like this, but I was going to be married to Peter. He often spoke of you and wanted so much to see you. So I hope you won't mind me coming instead."

" Our first meeting might have been rather embarrassing," said Denise later. " I was very shy and unhappy, and had never met him before. Richard was in pain of every kind. But as I began explaining who I was and talking about Peter, I felt a most amazing wave of understanding and interest sweeping over me from the figure on the bed. From the first moment I met him, he completely ignored his own suffering, and by rejecting it absolutely compelled you to forget that it was there at all. When I left the hospital I remembered only his indomitable spirit.

" The following day I received a letter written by one of the nurses at his dictation, asking if I could come again. I went. We talked almost entirely of Peter, until tea was brought in for him, which stopped our conversation as his hands were bandaged and a nurse had to come in and help him. I felt he might not like to be watched, so I slipped away promising to return the next day. I never knew why his tea never came again however long I stayed, until I read in his book that he had especially asked for it to be stopped.

" I went the next day, and the next and the next. We used to sit in the hospital for hours on end, discussing and arguing over every subject under the sun. He was kinder to me than can ever be conveyed in words. Letting me talk for hours about Peter, and then very patiently bringing the conversation around to the future, planning what we would do together, how we would write plays and film-scripts and books, and always when I left him I felt indescribably happier.

" We argued over everything, from the differences between faith and belief to the most becoming colour for pyjamas. Arguing, not necessarily because we held different points of view, but because Richard would take the other side on principle, just for the fun of the mental exercise. Even during those early days in bed his interest and enthusiasm for life were unbounded. He once wrote me a wonderful letter saying that he was now convinced that bed was the only really perfect existence for any ' gentleman of letters '.

" One of our chief topics was books. It seemed

PETER PEASE

to me that Richard was born to be a writer. That and flying were his two main passions when I knew him. He could put his thoughts—and mine—into words of crystal clarity, though he never stopped referring to us as ' the mumblers '."

This first stage in his recovery was intended only to heal his burnt skin ; after that would have to come the plastic operations which would make him able to go out into the world again.

He lay in that hospital during these autumn months, watching the leaves fall from the trees, the rain beating against the glass of the window, the small broken clouds drifting by, and the barrage balloons floating on their cables.

There was nothing else to do but think over the past and imagine what the future would hold for him. It was a period of incubation out of which the spirit of the new man was born ; but though he had long hours of silent thought, he would not surrender to the ideas which were slowly taking shape in his mind. He fought them off, but continually found himself yielding again to long periods of introspection, and thus without knowing it was making firm the foundation on which his final act of sacrifice was to be based.

★

In those brilliant chapters of *The Last Enemy*, " The Beauty Shop " and " The Last of the Long-Haired

Boys ", Richard has described his hospital experiences when Mr. McIndoe's skill rebuilt his face and hands. The hospital was at East Grinstead, in Sussex, and the Convalescent Home, to which he first went, and where he lived between operations, was the home of Mr. and Mrs. A. J. Dewar, Dutton Homestall, which they had generously given to the R.A.F. during the war. The hospital and the Dewars' house were about two miles apart. The huts in the grounds of the hospital were put up at the beginning of the war to take care of casualties, and these in the winter of 1940 were filled with R.A.F. wounded.

The hospital was presided over by Mr. Archibald McIndoe, who for some time before the war had worked with Sir Harold Gillies, and had been appointed in 1939 chief plastic surgeon to the R.A.F. Mr. McIndoe remains to-day at East Grinstead Hospital, which is now a much bigger centre than it was in Richard's time. Both the Canadians and the Americans built wings on to the original hospital for the treatment of their own pilots, and now, five years after the end of the war, it is the most renowned Burns centre in England. Patients come here from all over the world for treatment, and young doctors also to observe McIndoe's technique in dealing with this most delicate form of surgery.

Mr. McIndoe is a man of quiet reserved appearance. He is of medium height, thick-set, with a square determined jaw. A New Zealander by birth, he is somewhat abrupt in manner, and has a piercing glance. He could be severe with his burnt pilots, but also, like Doctor Johnson, he could cry, " What, is it you, you dogs ? I'll have a frisk with you."

When he comes round to examine the results of his operations, it is characteristic of him never to make any comment. The patient lies there waiting with beating heart to hear whether the great man thinks the operation has been a success ; only McIndoe knows how long it takes before the results show, and his Scottish-New Zealand temperament would in any case prevent him from ever committing himself to a prophecy.

Richard was only one of his many patients, and of all those in the hospital none more unlike McIndoe in temperament could have been found. Yet they became great friends. McIndoe must have felt drawn towards the argumentative and assertive young man. Perhaps he liked the courage which Richard showed ; perhaps the sight of the face that had once been unusually handsome called forth all the creative instinct in his art. Two years later, when Richard had left his care and had again become an active pilot, McIndoe used his great influence to try to get him away from night fighters into a safer occupation. In this he failed, but it was the only respect in which he failed, for it was his genius that brought the shattered frame back to a state in which it could be passed for active service once again.

McIndoe had seen Richard first at the Royal Masonic Hospital. Richard had been blind at the time, but he recollected the hush of respect which surrounded his bed while the famous surgeon examined him, and ordered the gentian violet to be removed from his eyes and saline compresses to be applied instead, with the result that he had shortly after been able to see. When McIndoe came a second time, he looked Richard over and then said to him, with a kindly smile: " Well, you certainly made a thorough job of it, didn't you ? "

McIndoe suggested that he should go to the R.A.F. Hospital at Torquay for a little while, but Richard asked instead that he might go right away to East Grinstead. McIndoe had agreed, adding : " I'll be able to keep an eye on you there." Richard had asked him when he would be able to fly again : " The next war for you," said Mr. McIndoe, and left him without another word.

A few days later he was driven down to East Grinstead. During this stage, when so much of his time was spent in bed, and when he was under the first impact of the shock of his own crash and of Peter's death, he kept a diary ; and much of what later appeared in *The Last Enemy* can be found here, written in pencil, when he was first learning to use his hands again.

The diary is naturally a franker document than *The Last Enemy*. Honesty and forthrightness had always been characteristic of him from boyhood, and the search for the truth about himself and his relationship with others had been continuous now for some time. His talk with Peter in the train on the way to Edinburgh had not been for the purpose of holding Peter Pease's world up to ridicule and contempt ; it was a genuine desire to set his own failings against the ideal he longed to live up to, and to reveal to himself how far short he came of perfection.

When Peter was killed, when the sea of pain on which he floated for so many months sharpened his perceptions, and when he was withheld from action and forced to contemplation, the search was deepened, and became almost continuous ; it took on the intensity and fiery purpose of the flight and pursuit in *The Hound of Heaven* ; and failure, each temporary setback, wrung his heart. Accusations against his own weakness and cowardice throng these pages. With bitter scorn he diagnoses his emotions, and hiding nothing from himself, realizes that his dissatisfaction with the result of one of his many operations is hurt vanity that his looks have been destroyed. Denise, mourning Peter at this time, had come to visit the great friend he was to have gone to see on the day of his death. The visits were repeated, and after each one the memory of her beauty and the calm of her spirit leaves a fresh impression on him. He is not aware at first that he is being unselfish in his devotion to her ; when he catches himself in this strange attitude, for the first time in his disordered and selfish emotional affairs, suddenly a beam of light seems to irradiate the blackness around him ; it dies away, but not without leaving the memory of its glow on the retina of his mind.

His first task is to understand the meaning and purpose of pain. Others beside himself are enduring stoically the same agony which absorbs his attention, and he marvels at their courage and records it, feeling very ashamed of himself for the signs of suffering he has exposed to others :

> Edmonds' operation today. Both lids and lips done at one session. He soon came round after they brought him back and seemed as cheerful as ever, though three-quarters of his face is covered with bandages. He has the worst burnt face I have ever seen and has been here off and on for a year already. His courage is amazing and makes me very ashamed.

Every detail is recorded ; nothing is missed by those lidless eyes, everything is written down, or rather drawn with a pencil held like a shepherd's staff in the left hand, blanketed, like the right, in bandages, but to a less degree. Even up to the moment when he goes to the operating table himself he observes and records ; and when he has come round and is able again to write, he reaches back to that moment when he lost consciousness and notes down the chaotic thoughts which gradually formed into a reasonable sequence in his ether-drenched mind.

Jan. 8. Woken up early to have my arm prepared by one of the orderlies. I decided on my arm and not my leg as this will save me the bother of shaving my new upper lip. " Preparing " consists of having one's arm and armpit completely shaved, sterilised, and bound up in a clean towel. We chose a piece of skin bounded on one side by vaccination marks and on the other by the faint scar of what are now my upper lids. I then returned to bed and looked round the ward, while waiting for the trolley.

Ward 3 stands about fifty yards away from the main hospital building. It is a long, low hut, with a door at one end and twenty beds down each side. These are separated from each other by lockers and it is possible without much exertion to reach out and touch the man in the next bed. Towards the far end the lockers deteriorate into soap-boxes. They comprise the furniture. Windows are let into the walls at regular intervals on each side ; they are never open. Down the middle there is a table with a wireless on it, a stove, and a piano. On either side of the entrance passage are four lavatories and two bathrooms. This passage opens into the ward, where immediately on the left is the famous saline bath. Next to this in a curtained-off bed is a little girl of fifteen, terribly burnt by boiling sugar her first day in a factory. She screams fairly regularly and always before being lifted into the bath : her voice is thin and like that of a child of seven.

As the time for her bath approaches there is a certain tension throughout the hut and suddenly everyone starts talking rather loudly and the wireless is turned up. For the rest, there is a blind man at the far end, learning Braille with the assistance of his wife, a Squadron-Leader, several pilot-officers, a Czech, and sundry troops, unlikely to forget Dunkirk as quickly as most.

McIndoe described this ward on Christmas Day as the most democratic in the country, made a passing reference to the mixed-bathing and praised the spirit which made the whole thing possible. I have yet to meet one down-hearted man amongst all these mutilated. Those with legs carry bottles for those without : men with charred hands condole with men disfigured.

Someone newly burnt and dripping with pus will be placed in a bed next to a man with a day-old skin-graft. Neither complains : neither can.

The predominant characteristic of the ward is the smell : it meets you at the door, a heavy pall ; a mixture of bed-pans and old dressings.

Sister gave me an injection at about nine o'clock and an hour later, wearing my red pyjamas for luck, I climbed on to the trolley and was wheeled across the fifty yards of open space to the hospital. There is something a little lowering about this journey on a cold morning. I reached the theatre, feeling quite emotionless, rather like a business-man arriving at his office. Doctor Hunter, vast and genial as ever, gave me my injection, shook me by the hand and wished me "good-bye". A dark green curtain rose up my throat and I passed quietly away.

On coming round I realised that I was bandaged from forehead to lip and unable to breathe through my nose. At about 3 P.M. Mrs. Tollemache, Tony and Pamela Mills came to see me. I had by then developed a delicate froth on both lips and must have resembled a rather "refined" stallion. They were very kind and talked to me quite normally. I'm afraid I replied very little as I needed my mouth to breathe with. They went about four. After that the day is a blur: a thin wailing scream, wireless playing "each day is one day nearer", injections, a little singing, much laughter, and a voice saying, "Naow, Charlie, *you* can't do it; naow, Charlie, you *can't* do it; naow, Charlie, you can't *do* it." After this, oblivion, thank God.

Jan. 9. Woke early in a cold sweat after a nightmare in which my eyelids were sown together and I was leading the Squadron. Mrs. Tollemache came to see me in the afternoon, and in the evening Morley appeared and took the bandages off my eyes. I was left with a thick dressing across my upper lip which pressed against my nose, and two sets of semicircular stitches under my eyes. I looked like an orang utang. Peering into a mirror I noticed that my right eyebrow had been lifted up a bit further to pair it off with the left. This was also stitched.

Later McIndoe came round with his Yes-men and peered anxiously at the scar under my right eye which was blue and swollen. He went on. There was comparatively little noise, but the ward stank and I was depressed.

He was a storm-centre in the huts; the "Mr. Hillary" who, descending from a brisk encounter with the enemy during the Battle of Britain, had crash-landed and gone to a cocktail party; the Richard Hillary of Trinity, who had taken a rowing crew to Germany on the eve of the outbreak of war, captured the Hermann Goering Cup, then gone with his crew to the South of France for a little rowing and relaxation, and then to Budapest to row on the Danube ; Master Hillary of Shrewsbury, who had enquired of the School Inspector whether he was there to inspect the masters ; the boy Dick who had appropriated the reins from his aunt and decided he would drive himself : this assertive Richard who had flung himself against life with the certainty that it would give way to his will, was not likely to be quiescent even in pain. He got his own way in the hospital a good deal, but now and then met a nurse who was for standing no nonsense, who fulminated and threatened, and either finally gruffly yielded or was adamant, at which point he surrendered with that small boy's charm which in the end so often won his point for him. Some of the most touching incidents are brought into the general account given in *The Last Enemy*, but some never emerged from the diary. Every incident reveals the intense struggle going on in his pain-racked body. His selfishness and self-assurance, his arrogance and egocentricity, had been burned away in the Battle and in Peter's death, but like his skin it had been burnt away in patches, and McIndoe could do nothing to heal this. The healing had to come from within himself.

He was being healed, but at this stage he could not recognize it. Others saw it ; his mother, who was a constant visitor, and could tell, though he did not express nor she comment on it, that Richard was emerging from the fire with a different character. Denise noted it : immersed in her own deep grief, she was continually conscious of his gentleness and sympathy. The first time she had met him, at the Royal Masonic Hospital, it had been only two weeks after his crash, but she had remembered " the wave of understanding and interest sweeping over me from the figure on the bed. . . . Personally I never thought of him as being noticeably scarred. His eyes were so piercing and blazed with such spirit that everything else paled into the unimportance of non-existence."

The suffering he saw around him at every hour of the day, and the full share he was bearing himself; the inclination, which arose from his very character, to think that what had happened to him and to these others here was just bad luck ; that there was no meaning in it ; that the thing to do was to get out of it as quickly as possible, to get better only that the pleasures of the body might again be indulged : these fancies and convictions all faded under Denise's calm eyes and yielded to the pressure of his soul struggling to be free. He had believed only in freedom for himself ; but Denise and Peter, " the two finest people I had ever known ", had dedicated themselves to a bigger concept, freedom from fear and oppression and tyranny, not for themselves only but for the whole world. " I was impressed ", he notes in his diary, " to see there a spirit far purer than mine. But is it for me ? I don't know. I just don't know."

But the very fact that he questioned it, even though he could find no answer, was a measure of the distance he had come.

★

It was a new Richard who came out of hospital for the first time, his features altered and his spirit different. The face was like a mask, like an actor's made up to play behind the footlights. At a distance he seemed the same ; there was the same jaunty figure, the same fine shape to his head, and the long golden hair with the R.A.F. cap worn at an angle ; but the marks of McIndoe's preliminary work were visible. The skin on his face was entirely new, taken from the flaps cut from his arms and legs ; where the patches fitted over the bone structure it was shiny and pink, and the seams of each different patch were plainly visible. He had no eyelashes, and the eyebrows seemed not so much a part of the face as stuck there by the inept hand of a make-up man. The lips were thin straight lines ; not yet had he got the cupid's bow which, in a position to petition the creator, he asked McIndoe to place there in memory of past triumphs. But the face was a masterpiece of reconstruction compared with the hands. The flesh there had been burnt away, and the bones of his fingers had been drawn down towards the palms. He wore on each hand a contraption like a small tennis racquet, its purpose being to keep the fingers stretched so that they could grow straight again, and he was supposed to wear it day and night. He records in his diary that he found them uncomfortable bed companions, and confesses that every time he went to London he had them taken off.

At first he was allowed out only a few hours a day. This was part of McIndoe's design for making these burnt men used to the world again. To begin with, they were allowed to go only into East Grinstead, and since everyone in the town had become used to the sight of these scarred and disfigured men, they attracted no particular attention and gradually got used to being with people other than the nurses, orderlies and doctors who were with them in the hospital all day. Then, after a little, they were allowed longer leaves and could go to London, again, to begin with, only for the day, but when they had shown no psychological damage, they were sometimes allowed to stay for two or three days. This was always the first shock to them. Someone was bound to stare ; involuntarily the over-delicate and hypersensitive would turn aside, unable to watch human flesh so damaged without an instinctive feeling of repulsion. The pilots' reaction to such incidents differed according to their own sensitivity. Some did not seem to mind, or if they did, bore it with outward equanimity ;

some became aggressive and were saved by their scorn for the delicate instincts of people not yet aware of what the war meant. To others — and Richard belonged to this type — the sense of beauty lost was so heartbreaking that they suffered in spirit damage which could never be repaired.

It was Denise who protected Richard from the worst hurt. She became, in the expressive phrase she once used, his "ghost-watcher". She was his constant companion on these excursions, and he noted that it was the attraction her beauty had for other people that diverted their eyes from his own mephistophelian features.

He never failed to record in his diary every moment of this new contact with the world. After one of his first walks he writes :

I began to feel myself slowly coming to life. People were interesting once more and I found myself gazing eagerly into their faces for some reflection of my own feeling. One or two looked at me with pity, but even this did not anger me. I felt no desire to stop and shake them and say : "You fools, it's you who should be pitied not I ; for I'm alive whilst you are dead." Often have I wanted to do this in the past, but today I only felt sorry for them.

I walked slowly along the Mall to Piccadilly and home through the Park and looked into many faces. Most were closed in as upon some dread secret, their owners hurrying along, unseeing, unfeeling, eager to get to their jobs, all making the world "fit for Britons to live in".

Poor fools, it's not the world that needs changing, but themselves. And yet there were some who pleased me, some in whom all animation had not died. I passed one girl, and staring into her face became aware of her as a woman : her lips were soft, her breasts firm, her legs long and graceful. It is many a month since any woman has aroused me, and I was pleased. I smiled at her and she smiled back, a nice friendly smile. I dared not speak to her for fear her voice would break the spell, but walked back to lunch on air.

The sun was still shining when the train arrived at East Grinstead, where I found a taxi at once and arrived back at Dutton at peace with the world. Even the inmates seemed less wax-like than usual.

*

Whenever he came to London he went either to his parents' flat in Knightsbridge or to Denise's house in Eaton Place. Denise had become a senior commander in the A.T.S. and was working at the War Office. Whenever she was off duty, she spent her time with him, and one catches a glimpse of these two young figures, both from his own diary and her account, walking about the London of those dark days talking of everything under the sun ; he comforting her in her continuing grief, and she with loving solicitude re-accustoming him to life, and trying to help him to interpret the deep emotion that was about to revolutionize his whole outlook.

Were they in love with each other ? The question

must be asked, and some answer must be given. Richard, I am sure, was in love with Denise, but she had not grown used to life again after Peter's death. Her religious feelings had always been deep, and after the tragedy of Peter's death she turned for comfort to the source from which she had always derived it — her faith. She spoke with conviction of going into a convent when the war ended, and at that time she meant it. Richard, feeling life stirring in him again, and aghast at the tragedy of beauty content to be immured, teased and argued with her over this subject, feeling himself at first the spokesman for Peter, who was the bond between them ; and then, I think, falling in love with her himself.

She was never out of his thoughts, and he was hardly ever out of hers. Soon after I had got to know him, he said to me : " I want you to meet Denise — if anything happens to me, I want you to look after her."

Denise, who was beautiful, had an equally beautiful sister and the two of them lived with a housekeeper in a house in Eaton Place. Denise had joined the A.T.S., and Penny, the other sister, worked in the Admiralty. This house was filled with their young contemporaries, all, both men and girls, in uniform. There was a constant coming and going, and much gaiety in the air. But there were moments of peace, which Denise always managed to provide, when she withdrew into the quietness which she seemed to be

DENISE

able to create at will around her. Penny and the younger ones would depart in search of fun, and Richard and Denise would be left alone, with only the sound at night of the outraged roar of the guns, and the searing sound of bombs falling, and the shudder as London took the shock. Night after night, when the house had been emptied of the young men and women who gathered there, she and Richard would sit on alone, talking, endlessly talking, lost in the mystery of each other's characters, each of them conscious of the darkness within them, and trying to grope their way towards the light.

Richard records that often during that winter, when there was an air-raid on London every night, it was impossible to leave the house in Eaton Place, even to return to his mother's flat. He would sleep on a mattress in the basement, and in the morning when the all-clear had sounded and Denise had mounted her bicycle to go to the War Office, he would walk back through the deserted streets.

There are innumerable references to her in the diary which reveal how closely they were attuned to one another.

It was Dutch Sunday and for the Cabaret a young man rose and sang " Yeomen of England ", and then some song about the fleet which called for him to do a lot of " Ho Ho Ho-ing " and " Ha Ha Ha-ing " in a deep bass voice. After this a Dutch brass band fought a valiant battle with various national hymns and songs of victory.

Denise said it reminded her of hours of agony spent on a hard bench at agricultural shows. Finally a lightly clad young lady from Bali performed some intricate dances, which the announcer was careful to assure us had a religious significance.

[And again] : Had dinner at the Mirabel with Denise, Penny and John Davidson. Talked to Denise for hours : she has the gift of making one feel intelligent.

[And again] : Lunch with Denise at Scotts. She contrives somehow to look attractive in uniform. Suppose this is a necessity if one is a recruiting officer.

All the time he was watching her closely. He realized what she was doing for him, but he was unaware of what he was doing for her. He longed for her grief to pass, not only because he wanted to see her happy. He began to resent the ghost of Peter standing between him and her, which was responsible for her mourning and for his unaccustomed restraint. If there had been no Peter he could have made love to her, in the direct disarming fashion so congenial to him. But she was faithful to a memory. It was more than a memory ; it was a thing that still existed. " Peter lives within me. He neither comes nor goes, he is ever-present," she tells him, and the ring of conviction in her voice convinces him that nothing he tries, pity, or understanding, or brutality, can shake her. She is lost to him ; he can come only to her through Peter ; and he is not ready yet for that.

In that winter, the winter of 1940–41, he is only twenty-one. Those years which should have been a preface to life, the years of his childhood and as an undergraduate, he had enjoyed enormously, and he had so much looked forward to manhood and freedom and all that that could bring. And suddenly to be brought up against a ghost, to see beauty, which he had always loved, acknowledging with pride and triumph a compulsion towards a life of dedication, the renouncement of all raptures, except those of the spirit; to see loveliness and give it sympathy, not passion; to "realize" oneself, not by joy and extravagance of action, but by remembering and living up to the high standards set by the dead: this was too much to face. He turned away, as men have often done from the blinding light of faith, excusing themselves on the grounds that they are of the earth earthy, and cannot sustain such height of feeling.

. . . It was true that Peter was much in my thoughts, that I felt him somewhere near me, that he was in fact the touchstone of my sensibility at the moment. It was true that the mystical experience of his death was something which was outside my understanding, which had still to be assimilated, and yet, and yet . . . I could not help but feel that with the passage of time this sense of closeness, of affinity, must fade, that its very intensity was in part false, occasioned by being ill, and by meeting Denise so shortly afterwards; a Denise who was no mere shadow of Peter, but Peter's reincarnation; thus serving to keep the memory and the experience always before my eyes. While here were two people of an intense lyrical sensibility, two people so close in thought, feeling, and ideals, that although one was dead and the other living they were to me as one, yet I could not feel that their experience was mine, that it could do more than touch me in passing, for that I had been of any help to Denise was in a large part due to the fact that we were so dissimilar. While her thoughts came trailing clouds of glory, mine were of the earth earthy, and at such a time could help to strike a balance between the mystical flights of her mind and the material fact of high-explosive bombs landing in the next street. But though we might travel the same road for a time, lone voyagers eager for company, yet the time must come when our ways should part. Right or wrong, her way was not mine and I should be mistaken in attempting to make it so. We must live how we can.

★

For sometimes the little devils of anger would leap up in Richard and he would be tempted to turn his mind from the questions he wanted so much to answer. Life would seem flat and profitless : " There was no future in it ", to use an R.A.F. expression ; people were kind to him because he had been injured, not because they liked him. He even suspected, in savage moments, that women let him make love to them because it gave them " an erotic flip " to feel themselves touched by his maimed hands. Then he would try to drown his misery by long walks through the bleak streets :

> Walked all the way up Piccadilly [he notes], going into each bar until I reached the Circus. . . . Drank too much and stayed up too late [he writes at 3 A.M.]. What a failure I am, and how I am wasting my life.

Once he went back, on the invitation of Tony Tollemache, to a guest night at Hornchurch, the aerodrome which he had left only seven months before, and found the place haunted by the memory of fallen officers, but he fought his way into the spirit of the occasion, and the night ended in a rag. Richard retired to Tony's bed and slept very soundly, waking to find an abusive note hanging over his head, and Tony stretched out corpselike on the sofa.

He tries to get in touch with his old friends. He invites twenty of them to come to drinks at his mother's flat, hoping to recapture the feelings of youth he had known when he had been with them at Oxford only a year before. But after an hour, he leaves the party and walks away by himself, conscious that he has lost touch with them and unable to tell why.

Always his thoughts were of the men he had known who were now dead. He was the last of them left, and it seemed to him that there was no reason for his survival, nor any purpose in it. If he could only stop thinking about the past, he felt that he would be all right ; if he could preserve the hard core of his egocentricity and think purely of himself, he would not have to bear the spiritual torment, so much more painful than the physical healing in the hospital. His repeated efforts to drown all thought are pitiful to read, because the remorse that comes is always accompanied by the nagging question as to why he should have lived and the others died. So sensitive has he come to be on this point that he cannot bear expressions like "This island fortress" and "Battle for democracy". Anything that touches on sentiment or feeling he recoils from as though his raw skin or lidless eyes had been whipped by a cold wind. The attitude is psychological, but it has altered Richard's character. He builds with endless care the hard shell of his selfishness, and then suddenly it is cracked by an awareness of the unceasing struggle in which human beings are engaged.

One night, as though the period of incubation had been fulfilled, the war and humanity finally broke asunder the shell of egocentricity in which he had tried so desperately to immure himself. The scene, recorded with perfect clarity, is the climax of *The Last Enemy*. He had arrived at Liverpool Street Station after a visit to friends in the country, and as the train drew in a heavy air-raid began. He took a taxi for the long drive to Knightsbridge, but they had not gone far before a flare dropped, followed by a high-explosive bomb which sent glass scattering across the street ahead of the car. He and the driver got out and went into the "George and Dragon", and as they stood there drinking a glass of beer, a stick of bombs fell and he and everyone else in the room was thrown flat on to the floor. As he staggered out of the building, an A.F.S. man turned to him almost apologetically.

" If you have nothing very urgent on hand," he said, " I wonder if you'd help here for a bit. You see it was the house next to you that was hit and there's someone buried in there."

I turned and looked on a heap of bricks and mortar, wooden beams and doors, and one framed picture, unbroken. It was the first time that I had seen a building newly blasted. Often had I left the flat in the morning and walked up Piccadilly, aware vaguely of the ominously tidy gap between two houses, but further my mind had not gone.

We dug, or rather we pushed, pulled, heaved, and strained, I somewhat ineffectually because of my hands ; I don't know for how long, but I suppose for a short enough while. And yet it seemed endless. From time to time I was aware of figures round me : an A.R.P. warden, his face expressionless under a steel helmet ; once a soldier swearing savagely in a quiet monotone ; and the taxi-driver, his face pouring sweat.

And so we came to the woman. It was her feet that we saw first, and whereas before we had worked doggedly, now we worked with a sort of frenzy, like prospectors at the first glint of gold. She was not quite buried, and through the gap between two beams we could see that she was still alive. We got the child out first. It was passed back carefully and with an odd sort of reverence by the warden, but it was dead. She must have been holding it to her in the bed when the bomb came.

Finally we made a gap wide enough for the bed to be drawn out. The woman who lay there looked middle-aged. She lay on her back and her eyes were closed. Her face, through the dirt and streaked blood, was the face of a thousand working women ; her body under the cotton nightdress was heavy. The nightdress was drawn up to her knees and one leg was twisted under her. There was no dignity about that figure.

Around me I heard voices. " Where's the ambulance ? " " For Christ's sake don't move her ! " " Let her have some air ! "

I was at the head of the bed, and looking down into that tired, blood-streaked, work-worn face I had a sense of complete unreality. I took the brandy flask from my hip pocket and held it to her lips. Most of it ran down her chin but a little flowed between those clenched teeth. She opened her eyes and reached out her arms instinctively for the child. Then she started to weep. Quite soundlessly, and with no sobbing, the tears were running down her cheeks when she lifted her eyes to mine.

" Thank you, sir," she said, and took my hand in hers. And then, looking at me again, she said after a pause, " I see they got you too."

Very carefully I screwed the top on to the brandy flask, unscrewed it once and screwed it on again, for I had caught it on the wrong thread. I put the flask into my hip pocket and did up the button. I pulled across the buckle on my great-coat and noticed that I was dripping with sweat. I pulled the cap down over my eyes and walked out into the street.

Someone caught me by the arm, I think it was the

soldier with the girl, and said : " You'd better take some of that brandy yourself. You don't look too good" ; but I shook him off. With difficulty I kept my pace to a walk, forcing myself not to run. For I wanted to run, to run anywhere away from that scene, from myself, from the terror that was inside me, the terror of something that was about to happen and which I had not the power to stop.

It is impossible to summarize the account of the struggle he then had with his own soul as he walked through the night streets while the raid still went on. All the thoughts which had been nagging at him since Peter's death and his own crash rise now like a battalion before him. He had so often managed to break through them, but now rank upon rank they stand there, an impenetrable wall, and after a long time he surrenders :

I stopped and looked up into the night. They were there somewhere, all of them around me ; dead perhaps, but not gone. Through Peter they had spoken to me, not once but often. I had heard and shrugged my shoulders ; I had gone my way unheeding, not bitter, either on their account or mine, but in some curious way suspended, blind, lifeless, as they could never be.

Not so the others. Not so the Berrys, the Stapletons, the Carburys. Again instinct had served. They hadn't had even the need of a Peter. They had felt their universe, not rationalized it. Each time they climbed into their machines and took off into combat, they were paying instinctive tribute to their comrades who were dead. Not so those men in hospital. They too knew, knew that no price was too dear to achieve this victory, knew that their discomforts, their suffering, were as nothing if they could but get back, and should they never get back they knew that silence was their rôle.

But I ! What had I done ? What could I do now ?

I wanted to seize a gun and fire it, hit somebody, break a window, anything. I saw the months ahead of me, hospital, hospital, hospital, operation after operation, and I was in despair. Somehow I got myself home, undressed, and into bed and fell into a troubled sleep. But I did not rest ; when I awoke the problem was still within me. Surely there must be something.

Then after a while it came to me.

I could write. Later there would be other things, but now I could write. I had talked about it long enough, I was to be a writer, just like that. I was to be a writer, but in a vacuum. Well, here was my chance. To write I needed two things, a subject and a public. Now I knew well enough my subject. I would write of these men, of Peter and of the others. I would write for them and would write with them. They would be at my side. And to whom would I address this book, to whom would I be speaking when I spoke of these men ? And that, too, I knew. To Humanity, for Humanity must be the public of any book. Yes, that despised Humanity which I had so scorned and ridiculed to Peter.

If I could do this thing, could tell a little of the lives of these men, I would have justified, at least in some measure, my right to fellowship with my dead, and to the friendship of those with courage and steadfastness who were still living and who would go on fighting until the ideals for which their comrades had died were stamped for ever on the future of civilization.

Chapter Five

THE shell was broken, and a new Richard emerged to take the place of the old. At first he found it wonderfully calming to the spirit, after months of tossing on the rough and restless sea of his reflections, about the past, about Peter and his friends, and about his own part in the war ; peaceful now to have recognized how superficial the old values had been, and to estimate how valid the new ones were. It is a moving discovery to be aware of one's kinship with mankind, to feel a sudden surge of anguished love for the human race. There had been such an upward spiral of emotion in England at the time of Dunkirk and during this fateful winter of 1940–41. Richard was only feeling with greater intensity what everyone in the country felt then, such an unutterable pitying love for the island and its people that the soul shuddered under it. In Churchill's graphic phrase, a white-hot fire ran through the nation.

It was March at this time, and the slow first fumblings of spring were apparent even in London after its winter of ceaseless night bombing. He was caught by a heavy raid while he sat talking to Denise one night. Walking home afterwards he notes that London in the early morning, the streets wet after a night's rain, and the air smelling of coal-dust and fog, is still to him the best place in the world.

Even the prospect of another operation on his face did not now depress him as it had done in the past. The change of mood is apparent not only in the record of his thoughts that his diary keeps, but in the strength and purpose of his handwriting.

> Lunch at home : two dozen oysters and a bottle of Pol Roget. This is what I call getting really fit for an operation. Just caught my train to the hospital. Saw McIndoe before going to bed and asked to be first on his list. Can't help feeling that the great man is freshest in the morning. But they tell me that he never tires. Has been known to operate all day, and finally at about 10 P.M. put on his coat, stretch, and say to his exhausted theatre staff, " Now let's *do* something."

He now wanted to get better in order to fly again. He was burning to write, but knowing what he wanted to write about, and not content to write only about the past, he wanted to immerse himself again in the brotherhood of the R.A.F. A new conception of heroism had seized his mind. It was personified in Peter Pease ; a figure and a character like Peter's, but not with Peter's face, for Peter was dead, and the new conception was alive, shining with life, and eager with the urgency of its purpose. The purpose, to defeat the falseness, the hardness, the soullessness that had its roots in Nazi Germany but spread its branches over the world. Under its shade some Englishmen were gathered, and men of every race ; those all over the world who thought themselves superior to other men, who prided themselves on advantages which others had not, who scorned the suffering of humanity, who believed that there was a privileged class. Peter had had everything that this world could offer, yet was conscious of his responsibilities. His attitude was entirely unselfish ; Richard's had been concerned only with himself. And the others who had not had even his advantages. . . . " The Carburys and the Berrys, the tough practical men who had come up the hard way, who were not fighting this war for any philosophical principles or economic ideals ; who, unlike the average Oxford undergraduate, were not flying for aesthetic reasons, but because of an instinctive knowledge that this was the job for which they were most suited. These were the men who had blasted and would continue to blast the Luftwaffe out of the sky . . . instinctively, inarticulately, they too were fighting for the things that Peter had died to preserve."

And had he been? If he had been left without an alternative purpose, Richard in his new frame of mind would have been passing through an agonizing time. But instead he bore his continual pain, supported by his new sense of oneness with humanity, his new awareness of humility, and the blaze of understanding which had lit his mind, after long watching the sufferings of Edmonds, and after the bombed woman had drawn him into the fold of those who had the right to wear the badge of common humanity. Edmonds had always been cheerful, and had treated him as a fellow sufferer, and because Edmonds had not been one of the Oxford brethren Richard had been unaware of him. The woman in the bombed house had not marked the signs of his upbringing, but had recognized the badge of their common suffering ; she, like Edmonds, had taken for granted that they were united in a fellowship of enormous patient mutuality.

That was heroic, and with all his heart and soul he yearned to deserve now this companionship that had been offered to him. Not to lie in hospital, and with undergraduate wit tease the nurses ; not to sit in night-clubs, battle-scarred in the latest mode, and with sardonic quips belittle humanity ; not to satisfy the desires of women who found in mutilation an erotic novelty : but to submerge his suffering in that which all humanity had to bear, and earn the right to share in its nobility.

The still sad music of humanity had sounded in his ear, and the note held, its soft sweet strain drawn out and perpetual ever afterwards. In another age, even at another time in this one, he might have found in some religious order a way of self-immolation. But the world was an arena red with battle, and mankind was striving for survival in it ; and there was no way for him but the way that led through this fire. His struggle to return to it now began.

★

He began to write in earnest, and completed the first chapter of *The Last Enemy*. Patricia Hollander, who was doing admirable work at the East Grinstead Hospital, brought him to see me one afternoon. This was my first meeting with Richard. I knew from Pat Hollander's description, when she spoke to me on the telephone, making the appointment, that he was mutilated, but I was shocked at first glimpse of him by the ravages which the flames had made. It was a cold afternoon in March. The sharp wind had whipped colour into his face, but under the new skin it did not glow : it pressed against the thin surface, as though only the crushed lines of the patches held it on, and a touch, a rough movement, might release it. It looked very painful, and the lidless eyes, which had had no protection against the wind, were watering ; it was as though at a moment before he had had an accident, and the anguish was still being felt. All this was sensed as he stood in the doorway and I greeted Pat Hollander.

Then, as she introduced me to him, I found myself

fixed by a pair of blue eyes in which a strange light glowed, a light which gave me the quick impression of being fed by an amusement which could only just be contained. I found myself smiling in return, and the first embarrassment of our meeting was over.

Patricia Hollander explained that Richard wanted to write a book of his experiences, and that he had already written the first chapter, which he would like to read to me. A publisher naturally shies away from having scraps of work read to him ; I therefore urged him to leave the manuscript, and said that I would get in touch with him as soon as possible. But the blue eyes were fixed on me, and the bright smile was playing about those shapeless lips, and I found myself yielding, as I was to do on so many occasions later.

I did not hear him read the first few lines because I was watching his thin skeleton fingers, horribly raw in colour, without nails and permanently bent, gripping the pages. He did not read well. He was shy, and the nervousness underneath his domineering manner made the skin on his face flush, so that all the marks of the burns stood out like weals. It was a terrifying sight, but not a horrible one.

And underneath the bad reading, overcoming the distraction of his burns, were the words of the first chapter of *The Last Enemy*. It was first-class reporting. The chapter is all action, and to describe action well is something which young authors find very difficult.

RICHARD IN 1941

But nobody could have done this description better. Obviously if he could write the whole book in this way it was going to be important ; and to Richard, who was perspiring with the effort of his reading, and very red in the face, I said that if he would write a few more chapters and bring them back I thought we might make a contract. I told him that lots of people had the faculty of writing, but not many had the necessary perseverance. I told him that if he would write half a dozen chapters to prove that, we could then make a contract for the book. That was all he wanted.

My last vision of the boy as he left my room was of a mocking smile, though whether he mocked me, the processes of publishing, or the lady who had brought him to me, I could not tell. He had disturbed the room and upset my complacency, and what I fidgeted with as my daily task seemed for a moment or two futile in comparison with what he had done. Fancy trying to write, I thought, after that scaring experience, and while still suffering pain. But he had looked both persistent and restless. I had an idea that he would go on with what he had set himself to do, and I had a feeling that he might, as they say, really pull it off.

★

His diary records : "To London with Pat Hollander who very kindly took me to see Lovat Dickson at Macmillan's, to whom in some trepidation I read extracts from the book. He listened with patience, and while not effusive was encouraging: he could not of course judge a whole book on extracts, but how long would I take to finish it? Having no idea, I said three months, and we left quite optimistic to have a very long drink."

Just at this time he had another encounter with someone who was an established author, and who by chance had suffered temporary disfigurement and had had to overcome it. Lady Fortescue, the author of many charming books of travel, sat next to him at a lunch party one day. The diary faithfully records the impression this meeting left on him.

Feb. 15. Asked who was coming to lunch and was told Lady Fortescue. Cursed myself for not having read any of her books, but need not have worried, as she showed no desire to talk about them. Asked her whether she wrote in longhand or dictated. She said "longhand and in pencil so as I can rub out mistakes". I have not the concentration to write in longhand and find that one's thoughts run too quickly for one's pen; yet feel that if I dictate to a shorthand-typist I shan't be able to think of a thing to say. L. F. tells me she has taken a delightful cottage, surrounded by small pools fed by waterfalls. Has called it "Many Waters" and asked me to go and see her there. . . .

Feb. 27. For the last few days I have been unable to concentrate on anything, but today Miss Wagg motored me out to see Lady Fortescue, and as I had hoped, I was not disappointed.

She has taken the most delightful cottage, set in an enchanted valley of trees and waterfalls and approached by a single precipitous path. Slithering my way through the wet leaves, I came half-way down to a gate marked "private", beyond which in the distance I could see a large red stucco house. For a moment my heart sank, then, remembering *Perfume from Provence* [which he had by then read], I breathed again. The authoress of that book . . . ? No, it just wasn't possible.

I walked on; and round the next bend I found my reward. Like proud courtiers, streams of cascading water poured down from the wooded hills, to subside in respectful homage in the quiet pools around the cottage. It was enchanting; and no mere trick of light and shade for I could not have chosen a more miserable day for my visit, with a thin driving rain blowing across the hills, and a white mist hanging over the water.

I rang the bell, in some fear that the good lady had forgotten; but the door opened, and she welcomed me like an old friend. First I was shown the cottage which should be priceless for the view from the bedroom alone, and then we made our own tea, toasting buns at the fire.

I asked Lady Fortescue if she had heard Hilaire Belloc's epigram:

> "The devil, having nothing else to do,
> Tempted my Lady Fortescue.
> My lady, tempted by a private whim,
> To his extreme annoyance, tempted him." [1]

---

[1] Richard seems freely to have adapted Hilaire Belloc's

> "The Devil, having nothing else to do,
> Went off to tempt My Lady Poltagrue.
> My Lady, tempted by a private whim,
> To his extreme annoyance, tempted him."

She sat back, stretched out her legs (clad in blue slacks) and roared with laughter ; from which I gathered that the answer was " No ". After this she talked ; of the lovely house which she and her husband had built together in Provence ; of his death and how she tried to live there alone, but could not ; and how she built " Sunset House " ; of her leaving France after the débâcle and taking this cottage " to be alone and lick her wounds ".

As she talked of Provence her face grew animated and it was not long before I found myself upstairs in the midst of a pile of photographs ; views of the house, of their " bergerie " up in the Alps, to which they escaped when the Midi became too hot ; of their carpets of narcissi ; of magic-scented tobacco plant bursting in fertile abundance everywhere ; and finally of the sky in the Alps, lowering and heavy before a storm, and fleeced with white streaks of trailing glory in the ensuing peace.

It seemed but five minutes since my arrival when the bell rang, and there stood the estimable Mr. Baker, perspiring but triumphant, with talk of cars and imminent gas lectures, and so, very regretfully, I said " Goodbye ", but not before being asked to come again " very soon ".

★

Richard went back several times, and in the end found himself talking unreservedly to this most sympathetic lady. Listening to him she noted that " he was a rebel at heart ; that he was lost and floundering in a sea so troubled by pain that he could not see the truth ". She urged him : " Write all that you have told me ! " But she records that, wistfully, he looked at his maimed hands, and asked: "Do you think I will ever be able to handle a stick again?"

A year later, sitting in a clearing in some woods in Devon, Lady Fortescue heard of Richard's last flight, and remembered him as she had first seen him, "silhouetted against a blaze of sunlight, his back turned towards me, the tall lithe figure of a young man in uniform". As he turned to meet her, "he deliberately, and defiantly as it seemed to me, faced the full sunlight, staring with hard blue eyes and an uptilted chin that dared me, at my peril, to pity him; as though saying with Blake:

'Pity would be no more
If we didn't make somebody poor.'

"I knew exactly what he was feeling, yet it was an effort of self-control not to betray how much his appearance shocked me. That beautiful boy! For his face was still beautiful in line and contour, though hideously patched and discoloured by flesh recently grafted to replace eyelids, part of the nose, and the upper lids; the work marvellously done by that worker of miracles, the plastic surgeon, but as yet lacking finish."

They had many talks, and deep understanding flowed between them. She comforted him: "You will find that you have gained far more than you have lost by your disfigurement."

"I am finding that out already," he said quietly.

★

He had now, in the spring of 1941, reached a stage of convalescence which allowed him to spend longer and longer periods away from the hospital. He worked hard on his book, but the condition of his hand prevented him from writing for long at a stretch. He tried dictating, but found that the result bore no resemblance to what he had intended to say. While he was in this state of frustration an idea struck him, and with his usual engaging directness he went to see Mr. Duff Cooper at the Ministry of Information, and laid the plan before him. America was not yet in the war, but it was the arsenal from which were coming vast quantities of our war supplies, now being amassed again after our losses in France. Richard's suggestion was that as an operational pilot, prevented at the moment from active service, he could go and tell the American industrial workers something about the emotions of the men who flew the planes they were making, and something of what their planes were doing ; his aim, as he expressed it later, was " to try to make something living out of the job of putting nuts and bolts into an airframe ".

Sir Duff Cooper, as he was to become later, and Sir Walter Monckton at the Ministry of Information were quick to see the possibilities in this, but the Ministry whose purpose is propaganda must never seem to engage in it, and Richard was dangerously ardent. Fortunately Richard was still in the Service, and only the Air Ministry could sanction such a thing. Perhaps with a discreet hint from official quarters of the advantages that might accrue, the Air Ministry instructed Richard to proceed to Washington, where he was to be officially attached to the Air Mission.

He reached Washington at the beginning of June; and within a few hours of his arrival a blow fell which psychologically left an injury from which he never recovered. After one look at his face, the heads of the British Information Service in Washington said that he must quietly disappear. Men might work harder in the war factories if they heard at first hand from a man who had used the tools they were making, but the devastating effect on the patient, unceasing work of persuading America into the conflict might be largely undone by displaying to American mothers so dreadful an example of the ravages war might bring to their sons.

One grows used to injuries and defects, even to mutilation after a while. Richard, like other pilots, had seen the sensitive turn their eyes away from the sight of flesh that had been tortured; had felt the quick pain of such a slight, but had been saved by pride, which is a different thing from vanity. He had survived that first contact with the uninjured world, and had himself grown used to the face he saw in the mirror every morning. But he had been in England, where scarred men were not an infrequent sight, and had been amongst his own friends in a hospital life. Suddenly to be told that he was too horrible a sight to be exposed to the innocent gaze of this new world struck him a blow which in the state of exaltation he had so painfully reached in London only three months before, and brought with him on this mission to America, might have had the most serious consequences. But he had not reached that state by a momentary whim ; much suffering, much brooding upon the past, had prepared him for the moment of revelation when he pulled the bombed woman from the ruins ; something so deeply felt could not vanish in a moment.

His sense of humour saved him from despondency, and in the first letter which he wrote to his parents, dated June 30th, 1941, the shattering effect of this decision is hardly to be discerned in the description he gives of officialdom gripped by its own apprehensions.

DEARESTS,

I had hoped that my first letter to you would have been one of sensational success but alas that is not how things turned out.

The first day was full of promise ; twenty-five reporters and camera-men in the Plaza Hotel and a most satisfactory Press the next morning, which seemed to please the powers that be. I then went to Washington where I met the Minister at our Embassy. My pre-arrival publicity had been unfortunate as the story had got around the Embassy that a badly mutilated airman was coming out to talk to the chaps. Had the cable read "operational pilot coming out to lecture" all would have been well. But naturally enough everyone said that this was a psychological error at this moment. The Minister read my story, approved of it, but felt that I was on no account to be allowed to go around the factories as I should be unable to avoid lecturing to women's clubs. The situation right now is so tricky over here and there has been such a falling off in enthusiasm for the war, especially among the women and in the middle-west, that he felt that the showing of my face to the women of America would have entirely the opposite effect from what we had hoped. I pointed out that I had no desire to speak to the women of America anyway, but he seemed to think it impossible to avoid and was eager for me to produce my speech as a pamphlet and to do radio talks. This I was not a bit keen on doing, for I felt that if I ever was to talk to the factory workers they might as well have the whole thing fresh. The radio talks could come later. With this idea in view I took a plane up to New York to see Col. Donovan. He gave me lunch, together with several chiefs of aircraft production who were all in favour of the idea and said that the whole thing could be arranged without any publicity. I should be flown down, and a plane would be ready to fly me off again as soon as I had spoken. As I was going down in a purely technical capacity, I should not be at liberty to speak to anybody but technicians in the unlikely event of the story getting out.

Fortified by this news I flew back to Washington and within the next few days managed to convince Casey, the Australian Minister, Rex Benson and his wife, the Military Attaché, Beaumont Nesbitt, the Air Attaché,

George Pirie, the American Air Attaché to London, Scanion, our Press Attaché, Childs, and all the American women with whom I came in contact. This I thought formidable enough armament with which to go to the Ambassador. That night I dined with him and Lady Halifax and the next day saw him alone for half an hour. Unfortunately, the nigger was already in the woodpile. The case had been put to him from the Minister's angle; he had put it up to Sumner Welles, who in turn wrote a letter about it to the President from the mutilated airman angle. A certain Mrs. Clark, who is pro-British and quite useful, also, I gather from Bill Donovan, saw the President and suggested it was a bad thing. Naturally enough, the reply came back from the White House, "psychological error". Halifax having seen me said he regretted that the whole affair had gone to the President in that light and that he had a perfectly open mind on the question, merely not wishing to take any step which at this moment could have the faintest chance of mis-firing.

The Air Attaché had an alternative plan; that I should make a tour of the army air-fields, gain experience, possibly speaking a little on my way back up the West coast. Even this plan, however, has now been tabooed. As you may well imagine, all this has driven me nearly crazy, though I have so far managed to appear agreeable to everyone.

But two days ago was nearly the last straw. An article appeared in a Washington paper (though only in a gossip column) that made the "I told you so" brigade hop with joy. It went like this: "That the presence in Washington of Flight Lt. Hillary . . . is not as good propaganda as the British may think. In the great battle over England Hillary's plane was shot down in flames and he landed by parachute — with face and hands horribly burned. A plastic surgeon fixed his face temporarily, but he is still badly scarred. He takes it beautifully ; laughs and jokes about it, telling what a pretty boy he ' used to be '. No doubt he shows how well the British ' can take it ', but all American mothers who see him, even in high society, murmur : ' Heavens. It might be my son ! ' I heard a few of them say that last Thursday at the Sterling Ball. Lt. Hillary makes these women realise that war is a thing of suffering and distress and not the carnival for which they have been preparing."

The dawn however is I think at last breaking, for after the last attempt to keep me quiet failed, I sat down and wrote a series of articles about England for the British Press Service. They liked them and, subject to the approval of the head of the Information service, I am to continue writing for them and to do some broadcasts together with producing my speech as a pamphlet.

The last effort to keep me quiet consisted of having me sent to Boston to see a plastic surgeon called Quesanzian with a view to six weeks of operation. He was perfectly charming, but said that he had orders to keep me there, so I hopped a plane and came straight back to New York, thus prolonging the *status quo*.

In Washington I have been staying with Mrs. Raymond Lee whose husband is Military Attaché in London. She is quite one of the most delightful women I have ever met and gave me every assistance in Washington. In New York I am staying with Eddie Warburg and his wife who have made me feel like one of the family. Eddie has given me his office in Rockefeller Plaza to write in till things get settled and Mary has introduced me to just about everyone in New York, both woeful and diverting.

The American attitude to the war is pretty difficult to guess as no two people think the same and everyone talks about it all the time. However, I hope and feel that it is the momentary shivering on the bank of the winter bather waiting for someone to push him in.

[*Later*] : I have been to see Dr. Webster in New York, who is reputedly America's foremost plastic surgeon, and he is quite prepared to operate me in a couple of months, should the Government decide that it is necessary. Have now had a bar put on the signing of my name to any newspaper articles, pamphlets, broadcasts, etc.

Policy, of course, must move on pre-determined lines. Matters of enormous import were at stake in our relations with America at this time, and the Minister was probably acting correctly in avoiding risking a large issue by employing a means of propaganda which, while it might have been startlingly successful, might equally have been disastrous in its effect on the culmination towards which President Roosevelt was slowly drawing his people. Gossip columnists in America often show authority which way the wind is blowing. The Minister's fears about the effect Richard's ravaged face might have on fearful public opinion were confirmed by the paragraph in the Washington paper bluntly stating that "the presence in Washington of Flight Lt. Hillary is not as good propaganda as the British may think". Quietly he must be put away, and he was relegated to the British Press Service in New York, where he was invited to write anonymous articles for distribution to the American Press. But Richard was quick to see, and to report in a letter home, that " an editor over here has a great dislike of pseudonyms and regards anything unsigned and pro-British as phoney propaganda and nobody's personal experience ".

The story he had to tell must be his personal one. Unless he could recount his own conversion from egocentricity and dilettantism, how could he portray convincingly the achievement, and the whole-souled devotion to a cause, of the others, the Carburys, the Berrys, the Peases and the Waldrons, the Tollemaches and Agazarians, the whole pattern of English manhood caught in the fire of this terrible war ?

In the room which Edward Warburg set aside for him he found the release which the offices of the Press Information Service, dark in anonymity, withheld from him, and all through this summer he went on writing his own story, continuing it from the first chapter which he had read to me in my office in London three months before. Something else had happened at this time to spur him on. One of Edward Warburg's friends was Eugene Reynal, the senior partner in Reynal and Hitchcock, the New York publishers. Edward Warburg, touched by Richard's plight, not only set a room at his disposal, but telephoned Eugene Reynal, asking him to come and talk to Richard. While I was writing this book, Gene Reynal wrote me of his first encounter with Richard :

> Richard was the first person I had seen who had been injured in the war and I remember well the first impact of his disfiguration upon me. Needless to say I was attracted to Richard as a person immediately. We spent a long and happy afternoon together exploring the whole problem. He had with him four or five pages which he had written describing his being shot down in the air which was all at that time that he had set down on paper. I was greatly moved by it and told him that if he could write an entire book with the same insight and gift for handling language that was shown in these few pages I thought he would have a book of the utmost importance and one which would do him great credit. We gave him a contract immediately and through many conversations the pattern for the book as a whole was evolved. He was in and out of my house a great deal that summer while he was writing it and he also received a good deal of help and advice from Lewis Gallantiere who had also taken a great shine to him. Lewis had translated several of Saint-Exupéry's books and had given Saint-Ex a good deal of help in the shaping of them.

The Last Enemy took shape. It was a deeply-felt experience to relive in a country at peace the burning days and nights of 1940, and the companionship he had then been privileged to share. Emotion recollected in tranquillity is Wordsworth's definition of poetry. The images of the past, when the past has been deeply scored into the memory, live the brighter when they are far away. The frustration of his mission to the States, the knowledge that while the R.A.F. still battled in the skies — the toll of lives was daily mounting — here men were at peace and life for them was untroubled, gave to what he wrote the passion and the urgency which makes *The Last Enemy* such a great book.

When he had finished it he gave the manuscript to Reynal and left it with him while he retired to a hospital in New York for another operation which Sir Duff Cooper, on his way through to the Far East, arranged for him. When he emerged from hospital the American publishers were well on with the printing ; and proceeded with such speed that by the time Richard could get a passage back to England they had already set up the book and he was able to bring a set of proofs with him.

Into the office he came one evening in October, just as we were closing. This was my second interview with this redoubtable boy, and like the first it was thrust upon me, and my hard determination not to be swayed by his ravaged appearance, but to be practical and politely encouraging, melted under his twisted smile. At the first interview he had read me a chapter which was the real thing. This had been unexpected. I had anticipated only another gallant attempt at authorship by yet another brave young man of the R.A.F. whose experiences had been so deeply felt that he must try to communicate them to others. Of these we in publishing offices had seen many in the first two years of the war. But instead of courage striving helplessly to overcome the barrier of the written word, I had heard on that first occasion a piece of pure, straightforward, graphic, memorable writing. Now at this second encounter I expected no more than a further instalment of the same thing; a promising thing, probably, but of no value until it was complete. And my mood, as I ran downstairs to see him, instead of inviting him up, so that the interview might not be unduly prolonged, was one of impatient fatigue that at so late an hour I should have to administer encouragement to one who might some day write a good book.

He sat hunched up in his greatcoat, his scarred face lifted to watch me as I came down the stairs, his long fair hair glinting in the light, his thin lips parted in an enquiring smile, and his vivid eyes gazing up at me; and I, in ridiculous concern with my own convenience, paused and faltered in my excuses about the lateness of the hour, and the possibility of our postponing until the next day a discussion of the book he was writing. His smile melted me. It was I who was ill at ease and he self-confident; this boy who was half my age and had lived twice my life soothed my civilian pettiness and put me at my ease.

"You told me," he pointed out reasonably, "to

come back when I had finished the book. I've done it. Here it is."

And from the bench on which he was sitting, from behind him, he pulled forth an untidy mass of galley proofs.

"I've been in America. I've finished it, and an American publisher has accepted it. These are the proofs of his edition. I hope now you'll like it."

I gazed at the bundle of proofs, and found myself speechless. One chapter six months ago, and now the book completed ; not only completed, but already accepted for publication in America ! What was this boy saying ? It was impossible that he could have written it in so short a time, incredible that an American publisher should have accepted it. Books by English authors find English publishers first, and we are instrumental, sometimes, in finding American publishers willing to take them on there. It was only yesterday that I had been patronizingly encouraging this young man to persist. Only a minute ago I had been trying to postpone having to submit to the reading of a second chapter ; and here thrust at me was the complete work.

Richard sensed the advantage he had over me. There came from him, I well remember, a little burst of mocking laughter.

"You seem surprised," he said. "Saint-Exupéry read it in America and liked it. He took me to his publisher who made a contract for it. I hope you'll like it too. Telephone me when you've read it."

And with a wave of his hand, and a "goodnight", he went through the door, leaving me there with that mass of proofs in my hands, and a conviction, swiftly forming, that this young man whom I had seen only twice was unpredictable, and that I should need, in my dealings with him, to be wary of being caught at a disadvantage.

Chapter Six

THE generation of young men who had to meet the second calamity of this century did so in no mood of unquestioning heroism, as their fathers in 1914 had done. Although at Oxford in 1933 there had been a majority at the Union against fighting for King and country, the anticipated moment having arrived, they and their brothers everywhere responded promptly, even enthusiastically. But they were explicit in denying idealism as their motive. They went for adventure, or out of passion with the Germans for being so continual a nuisance; they went because their friends were going, because "Munich" had been a cowardly relief, and it was shaming to have the same thing happen twice. They went in the great surge that lifted men up and swept them on in September 1939, part out of shame at the continuing spectacle of human degradation in the dictator countries, part out of exasperation with protracted menace. They went, not to do or die, though both might be necessary, but to get the damned thing done with.

This being the bleak and resentful spirit of the time, it was inevitable that the war should take a different pattern, even if modern weapons had not altered the form of the struggle. The men of 1939–45 could not have endured temperamentally such a locked tension as their fathers had known in the years of trench warfare. They were sharp, nervous, oversensitive, desperate, strained to a fine pitch, harried by the perpetual overcast of looming events which had clouded all their adolescent years.

From men of that mood came the pilots, the commandos, the paratroopers, the crews of the little ships, the troops of the Desert Armies and the men who waded through the surf to the beaches of Normandy. Every man amongst the millions was an individual, with a chance at some time of individual combat and action, and his temper was suited to the form which the struggle was to take.

It was quickly apparent that the great virtue of the manuscript which Richard left with me was that it so faithfully reflected that mood. And remembering our two meetings, I thought that I recognized that in his personal bearing, as well as in what he had written, he reflected it too. He was the exemplar of his kind. It was a violent, assailing, slinging temper, and it was at the same time an armour, the breastplate that protected against hurt the heart of youth. He had thrust his story into my hands, coming upon me late in the evening, acting on a sudden impulse. No doubt he meant in due course to present his book to a publisher, and since I was the one with whom he had made a contact, it would eventually have reached my firm. But something in his temperament made him come as the office was closing one evening, thrust it at me and walk away ; and his twisted grin under his peaked cap as he pushed through the doorway into the gathering darkness came at me as derision. But whether he derided me, or the process of publishing, or the work of his hands which I stood holding, I could not tell.

I could not tell at the time. But now the pattern seems clear. Soon I got to know him well and saw him for an hour or so every day. What he did with his other hours I now know too, for before me as I write are all the records : his diaries, the accounts of his friends, his love story, the final battle that he had to face, and the record he keeps of his dying up to the moment of his death. All these records are consistent in the reflection they give of his character and temperament. He thrust himself with desperation against the unknown, as if sardonically he distrusted his courage and must continually be putting it to the test, and all the time scoffed at his endeavours in order to hide his exasperation with the disorderliness of life. This was the mood of modern man. Though *The Last Enemy* is the story of his own experience, its mood is the mood of all the boys of his age, caught up in the crisis of the world. Hardly a word of hatred for the enemy appears in it ; a little contempt, a little mockery, and that is all. The disaster that has happened to the world is not due to the failure of statesmen to reach agreement with one another or the aggressiveness of the Germans, but mankind's lack of pity and its false values.

Richard's story is that of one of the "long-haired boys", carefully groomed product of Public School and University, aloof from the common run of humanity, a self-sufficient being, sustained by his share in an exclusive companionship which provided its participants with a consciousness of their superiority in birth, breeding, training, intelligence and manners. They were knights of an exclusive Round Table who accepted the text of *noblesse oblige*, but limited the practice to each other and each other's friends. This exclusive band of brothers was thrown into the war and embraced the Royal Air Force as most appropriate to their idea of sport; and in the Battle of Britain found the reality that any man may be noble, in despite of birth, and that courage and character can flourish outside the ancient walls of Public Schools and Universities. Richard, who was amongst the few survivors of that battle, had brooded on this long in hospital, had remembered Peter Pease's words while watching the suffering of Edmonds; had struggled against the acceptance of a doctrine so much the antithesis of all that his training had led him to assume; and at the simple phrase of a dying woman had had this cloak of concealment pulled away from him, and had stood at first shivering and appalled on the brink of his discovery. Then had come a realization of the task to which he would dedicate himself. " I would write of these men, of Peter and of the others. I would write for them and would write with them. They would be at my side. And to whom would I address this book, to whom would I be speaking when I spoke of these men ? And that, too, I knew. To Humanity, for Humanity must be the public of any book. Yes, that despised Humanity which I had so scorned and ridiculed to Peter."

His function was clear to him, but it did not alter his attitude. He would write from the heart. But his generation had been much frustrated and deceived, and protected the sore spot against further hurt by a sardonic expression which would hide the result of it if hurt had to be endured. Richard's attitude remained sardonic. In *The Last Enemy* he had attested the faith of the men who had died. In the short interval of life that remained to him, his sharp and critical eye seemed perpetually to hover over Humanity to see that it deserved the sacrifice which had been made for it. It is as well to remember this in the final estimation of Richard Hillary's character which must be made when, as the last of the " long-haired boys ", he went to join his dead companions.

★

It was not, then, my imagination which had perceived in his expression a suggestion of derision when he closed the office door on me that autumn night, leaving me there with his bundle of proofs. He had just returned from America, and he had now to report back for further operations or further duty. He had left America with some regret. He had enjoyed writing the book, and was sharply conscious of the contrast between British timidity which had tried to silence him, and Edward Warburg's generosity which had enabled him to complete the book. He brought away from America memories of much kindness, and of the happiness he had experienced in many homes. America was not yet in the war, but was straining at the leash, and it was encouraging to have seen at first hand the enormous reservoir of power which at some moment in the future would spill towards the Allied side. He came back in a spirit of optimism. Now that the book was finished, he looked forward with excitement to whatever lay ahead.

He found Denise still working at the War Office. His heart always missed a beat whenever he saw her. Her beauty was flawless, even when set against drab khaki. One of her duties was to go round the girls' schools of England, and lecture on life in the A.T.S. to those about to leave and ready for military service. The War Office showed inspiration in its choice ; the Service could not have been made to appear more attractive than it did when personified in this beautiful young girl.

But he found that she still mourned Peter. In talking to her he showed exasperation with her fidelity to a ghost, but secretly he envied it. Was he not faithful to the dead, too, after his fashion ? But unlike her he was not ready to turn his face from life. He was young still, and in his vigorous body there was a zest for living which could not be denied.

He had brought back from America a letter of introduction to someone in England whom his American correspondent thought he would enjoy meeting. Some weeks passed before he presented this, and then one night just before he went back to hospital for a further operation he called up the number given in the book, announced himself and asked if he might come to call. A voice, low and yet very distinct, a voice which attracted him immensely, invited him to come at six o'clock that evening, and just after that hour he walked into a room in which various people were sitting around talking, and found himself shaking hands with someone who was from then on to play an important part in his life.

Mary was older than Richard, a woman of character and intelligence. She had depth with gaiety and richness of mind which made conversation with her a delight. She had the gift of being able to draw one out ; the imagination seemed to be lit as by a spark from hers. It became easy to express one's ideas ; glimpses that the mind had had of some conception seemed to take shape and be realizable and understandable. Mary had the gift of sympathy, born of understanding. Comment from her was always valuable and stimulating.

I will not attempt to describe her appearance save to say that it was beautiful. But she had besides beauty a mind and depth of spirit which for Richard, tireless in his quest for the sources from which other people drew their steadfastness and serenity, was to offer infinite attraction. In the same way as he had been drawn towards Peter he was now to be drawn towards Mary, and in his last letters to her, set out at the end of this book, it is possible to recognize the maturity of purpose he had reached just before his death, and to see in effect the completion of the circle of his life.

To Mary, the first sight of him brought a pang of the heart. That one so tall and slim and fair, with such arresting eyes, should have suffered mutilation.

Behind a façade of great ease of manner [she records] there lurked a hint of shyness which revoked any impression he might otherwise have created of over-confidence. Only twice during that first evening did he reveal anything of himself. Once, when he spoke of his reception by our Ministry on the other side, when it came out in short, abrupt sentences, delivered rather aggressively. The hurt has gone deep, I thought. Then again when he left, asking me if I would dine one night. I was about to reply with conventional politeness when I was suddenly aware that his eyes were on my face with an intensity of waiting; waiting for a sign of hesitation in my acceptance.

She accepted, and a friendship began which was to draw from him the expression of much that still remained, even after the writing of *The Last Enemy*, locked in his soul. His letters to her, which I must quote at some length in due course, form a testament of experience which, if he had lived and given it expression in another book, would have confirmed Richard's place as a writer of extraordinary power.

*

He had now sufficiently recovered to be considered for further duty. He wanted to return to his Squadron, but it was plain that he could not be an operational pilot again. All that he could hope for was a ground job, or one at Headquarters, and to qualify for this it was necessary to take a Staff Course at the R.A.F. Staff College at Gerrard's Cross. Thither he went in January 1942, and completed the course at the end of March. His diary and his letters to Mary show clearly the state of his mind at this time. He was deeply in love, in the triumphant stage of love where the heart sings continual praise of the beloved, and the earth looks brighter because of the joy that possesses the lover. At lectures, or while writing "appreciations" for mythical A.O.C.s, the image of the beloved would suddenly glow in his mind, and he would rush away and write to her. Sometimes it would be a note of a few lines only, tense with the passion he was feeling; sometimes a longer letter would reveal the restlessness and the depression that even the fulfilment of a deeply-felt love could not assuage. But whatever their mood, the letters reveal a different lover from the one who had carried on so ardent a correspondence with Anne at Oxford and in the first year of the war. This one approached his love with humility, the old arrogance quite gone, desiring only to

> Touch her, like my beads, with devout care,
> And come unto my courtship as my prayer.

One of the letters is written on the night he heard of Colin Pinckney's death:

Sunday, 1st March

I am writing this just before going to bed and I feel a little sick, for I heard today that Colin Pinckney has been killed flying in Singapore. You do not know him, but you will, and I hope like him, when you read the book. His death makes an apt postscript and it raises in my mind yet again the question which I have put in the book and attempted to answer, of what is the responsibility of the man who is left. I say man and not men, for I am now the last. It is odd that I who always gave least should be the one who remains. Why, I wonder? Do you remember the quotation from which Hans Habe has taken his title? "A thousand shall fall at thy side, and ten thousand at thy right hand; but it shall not come nigh thee."

Tomorrow I shall go forward again, but tonight I have my head turned over my shoulder a little. And that is why I come to you, Mary, as I suppose I always shall. (I wonder if you are stronger than I?) For I want so terribly to convince you that I love you (I haven't completely I know) — and that out of all this death and destruction, not only of bodies but of sentiment and feeling, we may make this love of ours a beautiful thing.

And we have such a chance, so many things that we share already that now I must not fail; for if we do fail it will be my fault. There will be moments when by being careless I may almost spoil things, but if you will help me, Mary, believe in me, and be sceptical no longer, we shall come through.

God bless you, Mary darling. I miss you quite terribly and love you very much.

RICHARD.

The power of his love could not be contained. He had always been impulsive, forthright, aggressive, from childhood days on. The rapture of complete love which now seized and held him was intoxicating, and it stimulated these characteristics in him. He was a frenzied lover; she, I think, loving the golden youth of him, was older, wiser, calmer and more confident. She was also more intelligent and subtle, and knew, what Richard had not yet learnt, that love is a delicate thing, and can be destroyed by possessiveness. Gradually she was teaching him this, and gradually he would have learnt, for his notes to her often contain expressions of remorse for his aggressiveness, and touching promises to do better in future. " You see, this has never happened to me before, and I am not quite big enough to cope with it yet, although with your help I think I soon shall be ", he writes ; and after a talk they had had in which Mary had spoken of the perfect relationship between two people deeply in love yet always standing apart as separate individuals, he sends her, as an illustration of his agreement and understanding, some lines from Kelhil Gibran's " The Prophet " :

Love one another, but make not a bond of love :
Let it be rather a moving sea between the shores of your souls.
Fill each other's cup, but drink not from one cup.
Give one another of your bread, but eat not from the same loaf.
Sing and dance together, and be joyous, but let each one of you be alone,
Even as the strings of the lute are alone though they quiver with the same music.
Give your hearts, but not into each other's keeping,
For only the hand of Life can contain your hearts.
And stand together, but yet not too near together :
For the pillars of the Temple stand apart
And the oak and the cypress grow not in each other's shadow.

It was splendidly apt ; and I think that, written in a calm moment, it also reflected Richard's secret desire.

He could not overcome a lifetime habit of seizing what he wanted. A love of this kind was a temptation which had distracted him from the high purpose he had set for himself on the night when he had pulled the bombed woman from the ruins. The sense of dedication he had so sincerely felt after that episode did not preclude all other emotions. It was possible to fall in love, but — as on the night Colin Pinckney had been killed, as on the night when the Staff Course finished, and often as he pondered over the place and future of the R.A.F. — it is possible also to sense that he had an uneasy feeling of betrayal of the vow he had taken. At such moments it was a relief to have some reason for restraint in his love. "Tonight", he had written, "I have my head turned over my shoulder a little." Still the aching question remained to be answered: what is the responsibility of the man who is left? Relentlessly the question repeated itself to him, demanding an answer; and with his head turned a little over his shoulder, it was better to

Sing and dance together, and be joyous, but let each one
of you be alone,
Even as the strings of the lute are alone though they
quiver with the same music.
Give your hearts, but not into each other's keeping. . . .

On the night that the Staff Course finished, on March 27th, 1942, he made in his diary an interesting entry which reveals the state of his mind at this time.

It shows the cool, dispassionate view he could take, when talking only to himself and not to others, of his future in the R.A.F. ; and it reveals, almost unconsciously, how much he really loved the Service he so often mocked.

Today marked the end of a three months' course at the R.A.F. Staff College, three months of fairly intensive, and in the main interesting work. True, when asked for comments on the course, I submitted a paper referring to " the mouldy hand of Andover tradition which still appears to have a stranglehold on a College which surely at this moment should have as its aim the production of officers with initiative rather than resignation ; with practical ability rather than academic precision ", — but in reality I have learnt much and been agreeably surprised at the tolerance of the D.S. for my facetiousness, which from past experience I know to have been often resented. Most of the Air Staff have been down to lecture, and we have had several excellent speakers, but the two best, Hildred of BOAC, and Harris of the TOC, demonstrated that a lifetime in the Service is not conducive to eloquence.

Staff work of some competence is, of course, essential if we are to win the war ; and if it is to be one's appalling fate never to fly again, but to use one's brain and be responsible for the lives of others, then I think the course is as good as one could want. But it has proved to me that I can never be a Staff Officer. I am no organiser : but they have made a brave attempt.

I wish to Heaven I knew whether Archie's next operation will make me fit for flying again and whether, if it does, with this course behind me, they will allow me to function again. The Commandant, of course, does not wish me to fly, and asked me in the event of my having to work on the ground, what I should like to do, and what suggestions I had made to D.P.S. at the Air Ministry. I said, " To return to America ", but he did not agree. He thought that having already been once, what I now needed was responsibility. Air Staff India or Combined Operations here were his suggestions. " Think it over," he said and passed on. I did : for three hours I walked up and down and thought it over ; and I knew he was right. I had thought that this sort of problem was over for me, but I was wrong. When I analysed it I had to admit that enchanted though I am with America and the Americans, and eager as I was to do a real job of work this time, it was the possibility of collecting material for another book, of making contacts for after the war, that had really made me plump for America.

Having decided this I felt much better. I should very much like to work under Charles Haydon in Combined Ops., but I fear I should have little to do with his side except from the drudge's point of view. I wonder how many other officers on this course are selecting jobs with an eye to the future. A depressing number, I fear.

When I came back and told the Commandant that I would like to do as he suggested, he merely said : " Thank you : I will send a note to D.P.S." A very remarkable and understanding man. What a pity there are not more like him in the Service.

Last night there was a party to round off the course, and I found myself very curious to see what form it would take. The fairly old officers on the course are not by any means all regulars ; their ages rank from twenty-two (me) to fifty-four, and they were bankers, brokers, accountants, barristers, lawyers, artists and God knows what not before the war.

First there was a dinner with speeches, which as usual nobody wanted, but which as usual everybody enjoyed, followed by the inevitable beer, the bawdy songs round the piano, the removing of coats, and the roughhouse.

Halfway through the beer-swilling stage I came to the conclusion that I was enjoying myself, and that my former reaction to this sort of thing, first at Oxford, then regularly through two years in the Service, had been both priggish and smug. " Cats on the Roof Tops " was no better and no worse than normal, " High Cockalorum " the same, but when we proceeded to play tanks I really enjoyed myself.

Six rather staid officers of the D.S. behind one upturned sofa, and five well orientated gents and myself behind another, got down and at a given signal met with a crash reminiscent of Ashby-de-la-Zouch, in the middle of the room. Our future strategist behind our sofa then cried " Lift, you bastards — lift ! " and hauling up on our tank we sent it toppling over on to the opposition, who lay pinned underneath in various stages of decomposition and exhaustion, but blissfully happy. Bed at 2.00 A.M., or I suppose I should say 02.00 hrs.

And once again, a few weeks later, he breaks off abruptly in a letter to Mary :

What is the particular quality of the Air Force ? I find it hard to analyse. I suppose it is true that before the war, whereas the Army and the Navy each had a separate mentality — the result of tradition — the Air Force had none. It still has none, but it has something else which sets its members very distinctly apart from the other

Services. To say that it is an ethereal quality is both whimsical and untrue, yet I can think of no better word. It is something, some knowledge, not understood if you like, which can only be born of the combined humility and supreme self-confidence which every combat pilot feels. Perhaps in the end it is this. Any human being lies closer to the unseen than any organisation, but as an organisation the Air Force leaves more scope for the human being as such than any other. And yet if they do feel this thing, it must be unconsciously, for they themselves are strangely disappointing. Too often the theme is sublime, but in the attainment of it something is lacking. Will the time come in the days of peace as Mr. Harrison asks " when they will conquer something more than fear " ?

★

Meanwhile *The Last Enemy* was in active preparation for publication. When it was shown to Macmillans it bore the title *Falling Through Space*, which was that which had been given to the American edition. Neither Richard nor we thought much of this title, and we put our minds actively to seeking an alternative. The final title was an inspiration, and when it had come to him we both adopted it immediately. It was from St. Paul's first Epistle to the Corinthians, the 15th chapter and the 26th verse : " The Last Enemy that shall be destroyed is death". It was the perfect title.

Gradually publisher and author were brought closer together in this great adventure of setting a book upon its way. Owing to Richard's periodical disappearances to East Grinstead for further operations, the meetings in St. Martin's Street were at this time not frequent, but I met him often at the home of a fellow publisher, Morley Kennerley, of Faber & Faber. Morley and Jean Kennerley were living at that time in Barbara Hutton's magnificent mansion in Regent's Park. On Sundays the house was crowded with young men going off to O.C.T.U.s, or young men just about to join up, and I found the atmosphere, lively with the radiance of youth, a particularly pleasant one. Richard was often there, and the conjunction, so to speak, of two rival publishers, afforded him a chance for the exercise of his wit, and though this was often at my expense it somehow succeeded in bringing us very close together.

He had a great faith, I knew, in Macmillans as publishers, but it would please him to pretend that amongst the many Macmillan publications his own small book had been lost sight of; that Faber & Faber were undoubtedly astute up-and-coming publishers, whereas the antique and conservative firm of Macmillan, absorbed with their Kipling and Yeats and Hardy, looked with sharp suspicion on any newcomer to their list. Jean Kennerley, Morley's beautiful wife, in whom a sense of mischievous teasing was not lacking, abetted him; and sometimes, in middle-aged confusion, I had uncomfortable moments standing up to the attacks of both of them. But perversely this made me fonder of him, and somehow out of my embarrassed defence he grew to trust me the more. Yet I never ceased to grow a little agitated and apprehensive when I saw those piercing blue eyes light on me, and that mischievous glint pervade them, when arriving he would find me there, and enquire as to the progress of his book.

We had decided to print a first edition of 10,000 copies. But while this was being manufactured the Book Society decided to make *The Last Enemy* its choice, and we had to more than double the printing number. Richard pretended that this was but a ruse; that the old firm had lost the sheets of the book in transit between printer and binder, and had to go back and print it over again. Loud was the laughter which greeted this sally, and others like it which the irrepressible Richard levelled at his new prey, his publisher.

At this time I grew used to his dropping in on me at all hours. Our conversation was not always about publishing, though he showed an eager interest in the whole process and mystery, not only as it affected his book, but all books. He told me that he was determined to become a writer, and he outlined themes which he had considered and had stored away in his mind, waiting the day when he could commit them to paper. They were the ordinary themes that take root in a young, quick, retentive imagination, and I urged him not to follow them up but to write of what he knew, and of what he saw round him every day.

I thought that it might help him to meet writers who were masters of their craft. I introduced him first to Eric Linklater, and they became immediate and lasting friends. One night we dined with Eric Linklater at the Savile, and afterwards sat out on the roof garden looking westward at the chimney-pots and roof structures of Mayfair, lying very mellow in the setting sun of a midsummer evening. Eric pressed him to tell us the plots of three short stories which Richard said he wanted to write. The night being what it was, and our souls and tongues being free from restraint, Richard embarked on his exposition. The plots were interesting because they showed how eagerly his mind was reaching towards originality of form and presentation, yet how handicapped he was by his age and inexperience in dealing with themes of life and death not met with in the ordinary way. The first of his stories told by implication of a jealous child throwing another through the porthole of a ship. The second told of a wife watching her husband, whom she hated, about to meet a fatal accident which she could see impending, but of which she would not warn him. The third, even more *macabre*, told of a man who killed himself by fright.

Eric earnestly set about dissuading him from committing these extravagances to paper. I have listened in my time to few more interesting literary discussions than that in which an experienced writer, with more than twenty books to his credit, gave to a young man of strong personality and imagination, and a bright consciousness of the fact that he possessed the talents of a writer, an exposition of what literary practice should be. When I walked away from the Club with Richard at a late hour, I gave thanks in my heart to Eric for what he had done. Richard never forgot these precepts. Between then and his death he started to write along the straight lines of reality which Eric had recommended to him.

I drew him further into literary society by introducing him to Arthur Koestler, Elizabeth Bowen, Storm Jameson, and a number of others whose work he admired. Only five years had passed since he had told Mr. McEachran at Shrewsbury that he meant to become an author. He had " arrived " with this one book, and I was uncommonly proud of him. All his life he had loved discussion and disputation. He had it now, with minds as lively as his and much more experienced.

He was particularly attracted to Arthur Koestler, and I know that Arthur was to him. Though little more than a decade separated them in years, they were unlike except in one marked respect : the tall, fair-haired English boy in the uniform of the R.A.F. with his scarred face and maimed hands, and the dark, handsome, thoughtful face of the man who had been born in Hungary, brought up in Vienna, and in the ten years before had been in a Spanish death cell, had fought in the Foreign Legion, had been imprisoned in England, and worked with the Pioneer Corps on bombed houses. Utterly different from one another in origin, upbringing and outlook, they yet shared the common badge of having suffered in this age. Though they were unlike in all other respects, their eyes had the same awareness, gave the same impression of expectancy. It was fascinating to watch them in close and eager discussion : the boy with the beautiful, mask-like face, who had suffered physically and spiritually, and had emerged from the fire clad as a hero, but with the question he wanted to ask of life still unanswered, and the man who had trodden the road of suffering all through Europe, and was still in the middle of his war.

The Last Enemy, praised by all reviewers, started away in tremendous style. The book was published on June 19th, 1942, and by September of that year, even with war-time difficulties of production, had been reprinted three times. It was emerging quite clearly as a classic of the war. There had been a number of books by survivors of the Battle of Britain ; taut, hard, action stories, packed with drama and thrills. But Richard's book told very little of the actual action. It was concerned rather with the long, slow build-up, and the agony of recrimination and suspense through which a survivor passed afterwards. "Why have I been saved?" was the question the book asks. That was what men and women were asking themselves almost every morning in London after the raids, and the poignancy of that question caught at their hearts. He had found in his tale of suffering and his sad questioning the way to the heart of humanity. Not even McEachran could have advised him better than his instinct did in this case.

The success of the book both gratified and worried him. He took a boyish pride in his achievement, but was continually being sobered by the remembrance that his companions of whom he wrote were dead, while he who had survived to record their epitaph was making a great deal of money out of it.

He began to question himself. Was he hypocritical? Was all that he had experienced and all that he had described in *The Last Enemy* a phantasm of his imagination? Did he really mourn Peter and his lost companions, or had that been a pose, a mere literary artifice to make his story presentable and impressive? Was he a shrewd little beast, making money out of a good thing, with a sufficient façade of scars to make it seem genuine? He began to pass through an agony of self-doubting. A letter to Mary, headed "In Hospital, In Bed, In Anger", reveals his mood at this time:

Humanity is irony from the neck up. I guess that's the first thing you've got to realise if you want to fight for it. You'll get nothing out of it, and if you don't find virtue being its own reward sufficient, you have to be human enough to be amused by it, otherwise God help you.

As you see, I am in grave danger of returning to my belief in the survival of the fittest. ME, RH and to Hell with the rest of the snivelling half-witted bums that surround one.

I'm the split personality you think me all right, but it's not the poet that's uppermost.

I'll champion lost causes after this war. I'll write and I'll make people listen, but I'll make damn sure the sponsoring of them takes me to the top.

I was wrong when I wrote in my book that the mass of humanity leaves me cold. It doesn't — it infuriates me.

For example I know (don't ask me how) that if I could get back to flying I wouldn't get shot down again, I'd go on knocking Germans out of the sky until I was one of the country's heroes, covered with medals and written to by soft old women. But I wouldn't be doing it for them. I would be doing it for the sheer lust of killing to get something out of myself. It's no good, Mary, I don't want to fool you, I just don't believe what I wrote in that book — sometimes I do. I meant it when I wrote it, but now I don't. It's only when I'm with you that all the tenseness, the anger, goes out from me and I'm at peace. And you know, God bless you, how long it sometimes takes you.

It was just at this time that he was asked to speak at a Foyles' Literary Luncheon. Ever with an eye to the commercial success of his book, I pressed him to accept the invitation. He looked at me with a quizzical glance. "What's in it for the old crook?" he asked. "Well, nothing for me, Richard. We can sell the book without these adventitious aids. But people would like to see you. You've stirred their curiosity and wonder. This is the Humanity for whom you are writing. Talk to them about your Service life. Many of them have sons or young relatives in the Air Force. Tell them what it is like being there."

He laughed, but he agreed, and went away. For several days before the appointed one I worried him about his speech. Wouldn't he like me to read it over first? No. He wouldn't forget to turn up on time? He wouldn't. He wasn't going to say something outrageous? He wasn't. He wasn't nervous? No.

I told him that I had asked Denise and Eric Linklater to meet us before the lunch. We would have one quiet drink together to wish the venture well, and I would be very near him at the top table to encourage him.

At 11.45 he arrived at my office, perfectly calm and collected, looking very handsome, cool and efficient in his uniform. I was relieved, and celebrated my relief with our drink. Then it occurred to me how fortunate I was that this matter should have turned out so, and it seemed to me expedient that

Eric and I, who had no public part to play in what was to come after, might safely have a second drink. I looked at the youth Richard and at the beautiful Denise. I felt paternal, patronizing and happy. Eric and I were advanced in years, but the next generation, if Richard and Denise were a sample, were a fine lot. With a care to the boy keeping his mind clear, we did not allow him a second drink, but we indulged ourselves. Richard sat watching us with an amused look. I wonder sometimes what he thought then ; and what he thought at other times of our cautious reprimandings and promptings, our attempts to fit and shape for a successful career one who knew within himself, for his letters show that he did know, that his career was almost done.

When he rose to speak it was on a subject which I had not suspected he would choose. Who amongst us is a Fascist ? Who, examining himself, can detect in his conduct or his mind the stigmata of Fascism ? It behoved us in fighting this war to be careful of that taint. The young, clear, passionate voice beat round that crowded room. No one there had expected him to speak like that. It was possible to feel, in the silence and tenseness of that atmosphere, a thousand people searching uncomfortably and momentarily in their hearts and consciences ; and a stillness as he ended, then a great roar of applause that testified to the effect he had had on them.

Success had come to him again. The talk was reprinted in the *Spectator* and in *John o' London's*. I congratulated him, but for him there was no happiness in his success. Everything which he touched seemed suddenly to reflect the light of publicity on him, when what he wanted was the quietness and security of the shadows.

*

In July, a few weeks after the book had appeared, he had to return to East Grinstead for a further operation. Secretly he set much store on the result of this. He hoped that it would make him fit again for operational flying. A letter to Mary, written from the hospital, and dated July 2nd, 1942, starts " Please excuse writing. This is first effort ", and goes on :

I don't feel very well as I am full of M & B, but I gather from Rosie (who watched it) that the operation was a great success. She tells me that my lower lid lay for about half an hour on my stomach ere Mac seemed to remember it, when he stitched it on again.

I slept all yesterday — knocked cold by Dr. Hunter — for apparently on coming back from the theatre I terrified the wits out of the ward sister. She had visions of " Author of Hospital show-up dies in ward ". For some reason or other I could not get my breath, coughed violently, went purple in the face and caused general alarm and despondency. After getting me on my side and making generous use of oxygen cylinder, things improved however and anyway here I am. I'm rather sorry I missed it all.

Long letter from H. G. Wells today of which I cannot understand a word — also one from female pacifist shaken by the book. My God I never thought I'd get pushed into a corner with the unliteriots.

Last night I had a series of most peculiar half waking dreams mostly concerning you. One often has that feeling when one knows one is dreaming and yet remains conscious. Last night the process was reversed. The reality was the dream and consciousness though present was weak — most peculiar.

I have needed you and longed for you so much these last few days — with the body as well as with the mind, but now they are busy wearing me down with these filthy drugs. I simply won't let them near me with a hypodermic.

I don't see why because through you I have exploded my ego, I should not also through you find peace. If I cannot, so be it. But at least we can find peace from the stupid outer nonsenses which at the moment block the path of our happiness even if spiritually the future is strife.

Anyhow as I realised last night, it is you and you alone who mean anything to me : and that anything is more than the whole world.

And the next day he writes :

The dressing is now down and I shall probably go out over the week-end although the stitches will not be removed for a week or so.

I am really quite happy in bed, reading alternately *War and Peace*, *Heloïse and Abélard*, and *Jacob's Room*, which I cannot stomach.

I have an awful sense of time closing down, events moving in — suddenly we shall be wrenched apart and all the while we might have been together. I shall get a week's leave after this.

I am now putting the M & B under my tongue and throwing it out of the window, so feel better.

My darling, I'm sorry if I have caused you distress these last few days. I will ring you tomorrow to discover your plans and please, darling, don't have a crisis, or if you do, surmount it. I think it might be important.

Can you feel me beside you?

RICHARD.

Chapter Seven

SO many of Richard's decisions had been taken in hospital, and at East Grinstead at the end of July he took the most fateful of all. The book had been out for nearly a month, and the effect it was having was overwhelming. To anyone else it would have been exhilarating, but to Richard the fame was disquieting, almost shaming. Was this, then, the end of his high purpose, to be written to by thousands of people, praising *his* courage, *his* endurance, *his* ideals? Had he written in vain? Did they not see whom they should praise, Peter Pease and Noel Agazarian, Colin Pinckney and the Berrys, the Carburys, and all those others who had died for them? Were the dead so soon forgotten?

Lying in hospital, he thought of what he had done since that August day when he had been shot down. These operations. But they were making him alive again. He was the one to be thankful; it was improper that he should be praised for enduring something so much to his advantage. His love for Mary, deeply felt, had brought him to a new maturity. It was not in Richard's character ever to regret any experience he had had, but in conflict with the deep personal joy of living he was now experiencing was the inner knowledge of the spirit that something more of sacrifice was to be asked of him. From now until he made his decision to go back, this conflict never left his mind at peace. The resulting uncertainty of purpose was cruelly hard for someone of Richard's temperament to bear.

There began for him a period of intense frustration and doubt. He had wanted to write, but writing had brought only success and fame. Then he would return and be killed. But would that be interpreted as another gesture ?

He sought reassurance from his few intimate friends. From Mary, from Denise, from Eric and me. We all knew, perhaps better than anyone, the sincerity with which he had written *The Last Enemy*, and how deeply and sincerely felt was his dedication to his dead companions. We guessed the motives which were prompting his desire to return, and tried in every possible way to dissuade him. But when we opposed him, he withdrew behind the bitter, mocking mask, and turned the subject aside with a joke.

Meanwhile he became moody and truculent. He seemed to withdraw inside himself as though even his closest friends were not to be trusted. His letters to Mary lose their fire and ardour. The old jokes are gone, even the fiery outbursts of love are absent.

"You are there", he writes. "It is on you that I depend, but at the moment contact is impossible. This letter must seem ordinary enough, and yet I strain to be a part of you as I write it. I am not much good at straining."

And later :

In three weeks' time this posting [he was at Stanmore] comes to an end. Then what ? A momentous decision I know. And yet now it does not affect me. I shall go back, I think. I can rationalise no further. I must let instinct decide. Maybe it is for this that I have withdrawn into myself. I don't know. But this I do know — you are right. We cannot play down to circumstances. We must accept them — forget them, and wait. Need it be long ?

It needed some persuasion, even some deceiving of authority, to pass him as fit for flying. He was not fit, and any medical officer examining him could see that. But the Royal Air Force is an enlightened Service ; it could not be otherwise than unconventional with the thousands of young men trained as individual combatants with whom it has to deal. The Royal Air Force, I think rightly, had conceived the view that young men desperately injured in its service who craved to go back and fight again should, if it were at all possible, be allowed to do so ; that it was better to lose a plane and the man, though this would not necessarily be the outcome, than have a frustrated, nervous, psychological case, not injured enough to be discharged, carrying on a ground job, and infecting with his disillusionment and despair all the others.

They fended off Richard as long as possible. But in November, when he had been seen by several Boards, they surrendered to his persistence. Max Aitken had promised that if he trained as a Night Fighter he would find a place for him in his Squadron. The final Board passed him for Night Fighter training, and triumphantly in November he told us this news.

" And now," said Eric savagely, " you're happy, I suppose ? "

" Damned unhappy," answered Richard quietly. " I haven't told my Mother yet."

What did we all feel, hearing that he had taken this irrevocable step ? Knowing that it meant almost certain death we should have made outraged protest to the authorities, brought every influence to bear to countermand so insane a decision. But we were under the spell of Richard's personality. Something bigger than we was at work in this boy ; some power had seized him which had never entered our calm and negligible lives.

" I remember very clearly," Eric says, " the night when I discovered that I could try no more to dislodge him from his resolution for fear that happened. In his character — in his mind, his spirit, his personality — there was a quality like something with a sharpened edge and a fine surface, and I was suddenly frightened that my argument would dull the edge or tarnish the surface. And that is the sober truth of it."

That is what the Medical Board of the Royal Air Force had felt, and that is what I felt when on that winter afternoon he came to tell me of his victory, for such it was in his mind, and he was triumphant with it.

I felt a sinking of the heart when he told me the news, and must indeed have looked woebegone, for he attempted to cheer me up.

"I'll get a book out of it, Rache, and you'll make a hell of a lot of money, and be thankful."

But like Eric, I could not attempt to dissuade him. The decision was made ; anything I might have said would have sounded cautious and middle-aged, and to be contrived towards my firm's commercial interests. I could only say, "You fool, Richard, God help you," and be brisk in enquiry as to when he was to leave, and what his address would be.

*

I did not know until later what had brought his period of indecision to an end, and I spent much time wondering what sad and secret thing had subdued the bright Richard. I knew only that he was unhappy and restless, that he had withdrawn within himself, that he had temporarily at least become spiritually frozen ; and suddenly it was all ended, and he had gone.

One man by chance had solved his enigma. He

met Eric Kennington through Eric Linklater at the Savile, and they were immediately attracted to one another. Kennington had been one of T. E. Lawrence's closest friends, had served with him in the last war, and had perpetuated the familiar image of Lawrence in a portrait which has genius in it. Lawrence had wanted a portrait primarily to help him learn himself; and Richard, at this moment of agony in his life, when he was full of self-doubts, asked Kennington for a portrait too.

Kennington asked him to Homer House, and in a few days had completed the portrait which is reproduced in this book. It was quick, masterly work; as a portrait it is utterly revealing of Richard as he was at this time. Richard stared at it, saying: " I've got a face." Kennington had made no attempt to minimize the damage, beyond placing him in a strong light which emphasized the main form rather than the colour.

But it was what happened while the portrait was being painted that was important. In Kennington he recognized a man of utter integrity. In his last Will, disposing of the portrait, he described it as being by " the only complete man I know ". Some current of understanding had passed between the two of them as soon as they had met; and on his arrival at Homer House Richard said quite naturally: " I can learn here how not to play a part — and I've a decision to make."

Kennington found that his young companion justified the favourable first impression he had had of him at the Savile. He noted that he " could be a shrewd, hard judge of people, shredding them mercilessly — sometimes scurrilously, but who could reprove? When in a thoroughly naughty mood, as he swung his loose limbs and side-glanced with very bright eyes, so much younger than the surrounding made-up face, he was an irresistible child."

Kennington talked of Lawrence as he painted, and Richard listened fascinated. At night Kennington lent him his precious copy of *The Mint* to read. There could hardly have been a more fortuitous thing. *The Mint*, never yet published, is really a mass of notes collected while Lawrence was serving as an aircraftsman in the Air Force, and meant for a book which he intended ultimately to write. Those few who have been fortunate enough to see it say that it is a work of terrifying power; and by chance it fell into Richard's hands when he was pondering his decision about returning.

" It was reading *The Mint* ", he wrote later, just before his death, " that decided me to return ", and back in London he wrote to Kennington:

Two immensely important days for me: thank you for them. Lawrence, I wonder, or you? T. E. to some extent certainly, for *The Mint* helped to clear up something that had been worrying me for months. To fly again or not? I had got to the stage when I could rationalise no longer, but relied on instinct to tell me when the time came. The answer I can see now is simple. Does one wish to write for power — or success — call it what you will, or because one has something to give?

Again I have despised the men I have lived with in messes — pilots, too; despised them above all drunk, and have felt a longing to get away from them and think.

But Lawrence is right. Companionship such as this must depend largely on trivialities (the wrong word) — ordinary things is perhaps better.

That was in the middle of October, and when he came to us in the middle of November he had taken his decision, passed his Board, and had only a few days left before he must report to his station.

"Damned unhappy," he had protested to Eric. "I haven't told my Mother yet."

He went that same afternoon to tell her, and that night, November 19th, he wrote to Edwyna from the Oxford and Cambridge University Club:

MOTHER DARLING,

I just want to say thank you for always having faith, for not questioning my decision, for never betraying that you feel unhappy and, above all, for your unfailing sense of humour. We do not often speak together about it and for this and many other things I am so deeply grateful. I know what you think of my going back and if I were outside looking on I would agree with you. Yet I am glad the decision has been left to me. One can go on arguing the thing out rationally ad nauseam. I can write,

I am more useful on the ground, I only want to go back so that people may say " Well done ! " and to get a medal I am frightened of going back, I only want to make name, and so forth and so on.

Finally one must listen to one's instinct, and the time will come when I shall know that my instinct was right and my reason wrong. You must try not to worry about me and to have the same faith I have that I shall be all right, for I know it. It may be that —— has the inside information to which he pretends and that I am to be given something else to do. It may be that a thousand things will happen. I do not know. But that it will be all right, I do know. So please try not to be unhappy and lonesome. . . . I should not be at peace with myself if I did not go back. Afterwards it will bear fruit and I shall write. There are very few things to which one can cling in this comic war. To see straight and know where one is heading is perhaps the most important of all. God bless you always.

RICHARD.

The image of his mother, and anticipation of the agony he was inevitably to cause her, filled his mind. At this moment he was alone with her in spirit, and in the intensity of his feeling must have groped about to find some means of softening the blow which his death would cause her. He did not tell me of what he thought on that evening in the writing-room of the Club: what I recount here is the assumption which it seems safe to make on the evidence there is of the careful way in which he planned the closing scenes of his life.

He had said often to Mary : " You will be all right, you can take it." But a sure apprehension warned him that his mother could not take it a second time. " Both our hearts are breaking," he had wailed, when they had mingled their tears at their first parting. And now, at the last parting, he had the same sense of union of suffering with her.

He knew the way these things were ordered. A ring at the door-bell, and a telegraph boy on the steps ; or worse, in these days of no servants, and flats empty when the occupants are out all day, to return in the evening and find on the door-mat, thrust through the letter-box, a flimsy yellow envelope, to tear it open with trembling fingers, thinking, " He is coming on leave ", or " Oh, God, this is the end. . . ."

Sitting at the writing-desk in the Club, he could anticipate every tiny movement of that scene, could visualize every change in his mother's expression, and feel the utter annihilation of the heart's responses that would come if the telegram in the conventional phraseology of the Air Ministry " regretted to report " the death of a young officer, uncomprehending that it was pronouncing the death of two hearts that had been interwoven in a living union.

This was the painful part of the decision he had to make, and I know that it made that evening for him wretched. Finally, thinking as always of his mother, he worked out a rough solution which in the end was to enhance and glorify the tragedy of his death. He finished his evening's correspondence by writing a letter to his new commanding officer, giving him Mary's name and address, and asking that if he was killed, a telegram should be sent to Mary four hours before one was sent to his Mother.

"You can take it," he had told her, relying on her to meet her share of the impact of his loss, and then to go to his mother, and break the news before the Air Ministry could deliver their formal regrets.

★

All this done, the letters sealed and stamped, he eft the Club at midnight, and made his way through the winter night, and the black streets, to the flat in Knightsbridge. He went into his mother's room, as he always did, and sat on her bed, and joked with her, telling her of his encounters through the day, bringing the smile again to her anxious face ; and was content at last when her protests at his reported outrageousness of conduct had diverted her mind from the parting that was to happen in the morning.

It was a savage, a cruel war, and one's whole being cried out at times against the individual acts of violence. Already three years of the war had passed, and death had become a familiar thing. But it was not death that was the violence here ; not yet. It was the hours he spent alone that night. When I knew later that he had sat at his Club writing to his mother; and with that letter done, had drawn a piece of the Club notepaper towards him, and delivered on it his Last Will and Testament; when I remember the years of his suffering, the sacrifice he had already made; when I recall our too easy acceptance of his decision to return: then the cruelty of war is centred for me in an image of that scarred face bent under a Club lamp, the skeleton fingers tidying up his few small affairs. War is a monstrous tragedy, and if it for me is epitomized in the figure of that boy, preparing on that November night to join the mysterious exodus of those years, others I know have their own images. In your image and mine it is only the face that differs, and in retrospect even the face is only a golden haze, a radiance, a memory of young life.

These, who desired to live, went out to death:
Dark underground their golden youth is lying.
We live: and there is brightness in our breath
They could not know — the splendour of their dying.

Chapter Eight

IT was like returning to school, Richard thought. God, how he had hated those partings from his mother. Each time it had torn the heart from him. The past remembered like a lost paradise : the present grim beyond the imagining of hell. At night in his room at Charter Hall all the memories of first nights in cold dormitories, the sense of utter loss, of loneliness and despair, swept over him. In those days he had cried into his hard pillow. Now instead he wrote. It had become a way of easing pain.

I feel like a Hollywood gangster hero, who voluntarily walking back into the gaol hears the prison gates clang behind him for the last time.

First the journey ; I left King's Cross at 10 A.M. and arrived foodless at Berwick about 6 P.M. — strangely touched by a gesture of my father, who, after bidding me goodbye, came back with a packet of cigarettes. I avoided thought all the way up by reading right through Hesketh Pearson's life of G. B. S.

At Berwick night had fallen and the platform was cold, but the train to Reston arrived in after ten minutes. In the compartment were a couple of youngsters, fresh from training school and eager to get on to the course. It was largely to get back into communion with these that I made up my mind to return in the first place — but I felt outside, or rather not so much outside, but as though they were less fine than those I knew then.

At Reston we changed again and I went to a compartment by myself, and watching the sparks fly by I felt very low.

Finally at Gaveston we all decamped and after half an hour a van trundled us five miles into the camp.

It is perhaps the camp more than anything which is likely to break me.

The sleeping huts are dispersed over a distance of a couple of miles. My room has no fire, coal being scarce. The walls are horribly damp. All this I could bear if it were not that in the mess — such as it is — there is no chance of ever being alone and yet I am alone all the time. This is the end of the world.

The whole atmosphere is the one I dread most — emptiness.

Do you remember the line in my book about Sunday lunch at Shrewsbury — the bars on the windows, the boys crouching dispiritedly over plates of cold trifle ? This is the same.

The baths, which have no plugs, are in a separate building, though I don't see why this should worry me as I shall never have the rapid organising power to fit one in.

The worst moment was an armament lecture — an exact repetition of one we had at Kinloss. I kept expecting to look up and see Noel beside me, instead of which there was a pinched little boy who picked his nose.

All day my eyes have pricked with tears, and now at last in the privacy of my room I have been weeping like a child for an hour. Why? Is it fear? I have not yet seen an aeroplane and I know not yet whether the night will terrify me or not. Is it just the atmosphere? Very largely, I know. But perhaps this is what they mean in the Air Force by "lack of moral fibre". I have often wondered. Maybe this is what happens when a man's nerve goes. And yet, I am not consciously *frightened* of anything, merely unutterably wretched.

This is an awfully egotistical letter, and not much of a showing on my first day. But suddenly I wondered whether I should have listened to advice and not come back.

Phyllis Bottome said that it was only Nazis who forced themselves to do things, and that that way was unnatural for me. I should like to believe her now, but perhaps that is a mere bleat of fear.

Certainly my London period must have sapped my will, but I did not think I would break as quickly as this. And yet it is so largely the surroundings and the sense of being trapped, and knowing, almost for certain, that I shall not pass out of here till Max [1] has left the Squadron or until it has gone overseas — and then knowing no one any longer in Fighter Command.

I have been looking through the scant library here and coming across T. E. Lawrence's *Letters*, I took the book out, and, believe it or not, opened it at this page: Garnett speaking about Lawrence wanting to get back to the R.A.F.—

> "Since the period at Uxbridge had been a time of great suffering, one wonders whether his will had not become greater than his intelligence. . . . The courage

[1] Aitken.

of the boy too proud to make a fuss is something we admire ; in an educated man it is ridiculous and a sign of abnormality."

And yet am I now to go crawling to them on my knees, snivelling to be let out ?

They always regarded me askance — " Done no twin engine stuff ? Only six hours at night. Are you sure you want to go into night fighters ? Don't forget it's not only your life but your air gunner's." A damnably cruel but true point.

Perhaps they're right — perhaps it is the night which is subconsciously too much. I *know* I'm not frightened of flying by day.

Perhaps it is merely the fear of being so much alone — a bitter pill when I always thought I liked it so much. But the total lack of human contact is awful — they are machines, not men. At Fighter Command they were people. One could talk to them and like them.

★

But the mood changed, just as it had at Shrewsbury when the agony of separation had worn off, and he began to see qualities in his fellow beings.

The morning started badly ; bitterly cold, a long walk over to flights, and an indifferent dual performance on a Blenheim. Then this afternoon something clicked. My instructor climbed out and in an over-casual voice said " O.K. off you go. Just time for a couple of circuits and bumps," and I was on my own.

Round I go, twice without mishap, and am as exhilarated as after my first solo three years ago. I saunter into the mess, my battledress carelessly undone, and a voice calls out, " So you made it." They have been watching. " I saw you take off — very nice landing — the old ace back on the job again." So they are human after all. I feel a new-old warmth begin to course through me : the potion is already at work.

I pick up a newspaper — Beveridge Report ? Oh, the fellow is thinking about after the war — what do we care about after the war : we'll be dead anyway. Let's find out what Jane's doing in the *Daily Mirror*. We turn to the page — we comment on her legs, and I look closely at the faces around me, and what I see pleases me. I am happy.

We wander into dinner and afterwards we crowd round the fire, order beers, more beers, and talk shop. Time passes. Am I bored ? A little, but only a very little, for tomorrow I shall be up again.

This morning I was thinking seriously of asking for a transfer to a day O.T.U. — Spitfires again — easy to handle, people I know. Now I'm off on a new adventure.

*

As the weeks passed, he regained the enthusiasm that springs from doing a job well.

A sixty mile an hour gale has been blowing all day with a cloud base of 600 ft., so flying has indeed been a battle with the elements. Taxi-ing around the perimeter track developed into a fierce tussle between pilot and machine. One wrestled with the wheel as though forty thousand Gremlins were blowing on the rudder and tail fin. In doing so I took most of the skin off one hand, and as a result I'm in a lowering temper. And yet the whole thing grows on one, and in a curious way I am beginning to enjoy myself.

It appears likely that during the next two months we shall be snow-bound and any chance of finishing the course on time has already gone overboard.

★

" The whole thing grows on one." Soon he was to find himself back in the mood of 1940.

Yesterday dawned with low grey clouds and a driving wind that picked up the rain and threw it suddenly in your face. All round Dispersal, the ground, frozen only the day before, was liquid mud, caking on to your boots, following you everywhere ; into your plane, into the mess, almost, it seemed, into your food.

I was on second detail and had to do a cross-country. This entailed working out a course on the computator before taking the air ; a feat quite beyond the mathematical imbecility of my brain. Fortunately three others were on the same exercise, so I left it to one of them, a young fellow called Smithson, a serious-minded youth, without much originality ; but, like all the others, perfectly capable of understanding the (to me) impossible intricacies of a computator.

" You *are* a clot," he said cheerfully, and did his best to show me how it was done.

As soon as I was airborne I folded my map and stuck it away : it was about as much use as a sick headache and for an hour and a half I flew the three legs of the journey on my instruments in unbroken cloud, grey, damp and clawing. It's a curious sensation to be flying like that, unable to see anything, confined in that small space with only the monotonous voice of the ground control to remind you of the existence of another human being. I find it intensely interesting.

The wind was almost a gale when I got back, and unable to use the brake properly, I couldn't hold her, and much to my chagrin bogged in the soft mud at the side of the perimeter track.

I climbed irritably out and went along to the flight office to sign up.

My instructor peered morosely out of the window.

" Have a good trip ? "

" So so. In cloud all the way."

" See anything of Smithson ? "

" Didn't see a bloody thing. Heard control call him up once and tell him he was thirty miles off his course."

" Did he answer ? "

" I don't know, why ? "

" Looks as if he's had it. There's a machine crashed north of Dumfries and he's not back yet."

" Any details ? "

" Burnt out. Can't find the bod."

" May have baled out then."

" Hm, maybe."

I walked over to the locker room and got out my gear. Then I started to fill up my log book — most of the old times I had to invent, but I made a fair guess.

Confirmation came through. They found the body 100 yds. away.

The news filtered slowly through the locker room. One of the Sergeant instructors looked up. " Who ? Smithson ? Oh well, one a course, that's the average."

A young Australian pupil came up to me : his face was excited.

" I say, Smithson has pranged."

" What do you want me to do about it ? "

I went into the flight office to see my instructor. " Going up to the mess ? "

" Might as well. The weather closing in."

" Can I have a lift ? "

" O.K. If we step on it there'll be some tea left."

Koestler has a theory for this. He believes there are two planes of existence, which he calls the " vie tragique " and the " vie triviale ". Usually we move on the plane of the " vie triviale ", but occasionally, in moments of elation, danger, etc. we find ourselves transferred to the plane of the " vie tragique ", with its un-commonsense cosmic perspective. One of the miseries of the human condition is that we can neither live perpetually on the one nor on the other plane, but oscillate between the two. When we are on the trivial plane, the realities of the other are nonsense — overstrung nerves, etc. When we live on the tragic plane, the joys and sorrows of the other are shallow, frivolous, trifling. Some people try all their lives to make up their minds on which plane to live — unable to recognise that we are condemned to live alternatingly on both in a biological rhythm. But it happens in exceptional circumstances — for instance if one has to live through a long stretch of time in physical danger—that one is placed as it were on the intersection line of the two planes ; a curious situation which is a kind of tight rope walking on one's nerves. As few people can bear it for long, they elaborate conventions and formulas — e.g. R.A.F. slang and understatement. In other words they try to assimilate the tragic with the trivial plane. *Au fond*, he thinks that it is one of the main mechanisms of the evolution of civilisation: to petrify the violent and tragic into dignified conventional formulae. I think he is right.

★

He was caught up now in the Service life. The chief reason for his return had been to justify himself before the steady gaze of his dead companions of the 1940 battles. At last he felt that he was doing this. His private terrors, the fumbling of his burnt hands at the controls of these heavy machines; these were hidden from the sight of everyone. Preparing for flight, he feels the same excitement that he felt on the Severn in the years before the war, and in the huts at Hornchurch in the golden August days of 1940. He records everything now, as he did then. His eye for detail and character misses nothing. Night time on the Berwickshire station is as brilliantly lit by his description as the Spitfire strips in the Thames Estuary are in *The Last Enemy*.

There has been no moment at all in which to write or think in the last two days, for we are flying night and day. And yet somehow I must get this all down, these three months, even if it's only notes and impressions, so that it may not be wasted.

Yesterday's two operative words were "cold" and "bull". The Christmas hangovers were to be forgotten and we were at work again.

. . . The Boxing Night dance: [He was just back from a Christmas leave] "Do you live round here?"

" Yes." — " How long have you been at Charter Hall ? " " A month too long." Ha, ha. — Pause getting too long. " Would you like to dance ? " A smile. It finishes — we are still together — frantic signal to someone to say I'm wanted on the telephone. I've never yet been able to discover how to leave someone gracefully after a dance. I want to go to bed, but I stay on watching people getting drunk — talking of the " blacks " they put up the night before, etc. At 2.30 I am still there. Why ? I don't know. I've long ago got over that distressing emotion which should be confined to middle-aged women and very young boys — the fear of missing something — and yet I stayed.

But yesterday. Full parade for all those not on essential duties. Best blue to be worn. Squads to form up separately and march down to an empty hangar where whole station forms up as a wing. Apparently at a night fighter O.T.U., fighting time and the weather to get in flying hours — flying is not an essential duty !

Everyone must wear best blue — this means that there can be no flying all morning as airmen and officers alike have to get changed again into working clothes afterwards.

We march down and we form up and we wait — the whole station — stiff, frozen, until all feeling goes from my fingers — twenty minutes before the G.C. arrives, heaves himself out of his car and waddles forward to inspect us. He takes an hour to do this — the parade has no other function, and I stand squeezing my toes in my shoes, seeing how long I can stand absolutely motionless. The one nonsense — the other beneficial self-discipline derived from the nonsense. An ambulance is drawn up opposite the lines of men — our line outside the hangar — standing on what yesterday was a sea of red mud — now frozen solid. Why the ambulance ? I soon remember. Two airmen, green in the face, are escorted over to it. Nobody moves but the Padre and the Liaison Major — God forbid, no prayers — they walk up and down, up and down. The G.C. and his staff are somewhere behind. I hear a female voice say No. 8 Squadron attention, so I know that he must be near the end. Everyone is called to attention and he speaks. I cannot hear what he says, but it is something to do with Christmas being over ; shoulders to the wheel, etc.

Finally it is over. " Fall out officers," he calls out. We are pupils and it should not apply to our Squadron. I walk off — pushing the others before me. He eyes me but can say nothing. We salute and march away — stamping our feet, waving our arms, fearing the moment when circulation will return.

There will be no ground crews to service my aircraft, but those four of us who are on night flying detail must do a night flying test, so we get our aircraft and fly it around the aerodrome once — the others starting it up.

I go first, in a Blenheim I. I have never flown one before, always having been put in 5s (Bisleys) A. Squadron to save my hands. The Bisleys have a switch to shut the gills — the Blenheims a wheel somewhere behind the pilot that needs about 50 turns. The Bisleys have a simple lever up and down to raise and lower the undercarriage — the Blenheims have a catch out from the handle which must be pushed in with the thumb before the undercarriage can be pulled up.

No one has ever shown me the cockpit, but I think I can manage and I take off. I find I cannot reach the catch with my thumb. The ground control calls up — " Hullo, one zero two, your undercarriage is still down." It is indeed and I cannot be bothered to answer. I have to let go of the stick and am wrestling with the lever with both hands. It will not budge. I curse and sweat blood, but it will not come up, so I land again, very dispirited.

My Squadron Commander comes up. " Can't cope, eh, old boy. Too bad." Genially — " We'll have to throw you off the course. No Bisleys in this Squadron." Finally he arranges for someone to go up and pull it up for me until I get on to Beaufighters ; which I shall find simpler.

In the afternoon I go with my R.O. (radio observer) for an hour on the Link Trainer. This is really the only flying I enjoy here because it is warm.

At 4.30 we go down again. Night flying begins at 5.

A 50-mile an hour gale is blowing from the North, and some light snow is falling.

Then begins the worst part — the getting ready. No blithe leaping in and taking off as in a Spitfire. My R.O. and I go into the locker room and he helps me. First I take off my shoes and stand on my coat while he winds my Irving suit trousers, leather and fur-lined, around me, pulling and heaving on the zips. Next my boots — over the trousers and again zip, zip. Now the Irving coat. I struggle into it and tighten the belt around me while he buttons me into my Mae West. Now maps in one boot top and torch in the other. Gloves — these take a little time because of my hands. Finally, helmet R.T. connection and about a mile of oxygen tubing. I stand up breathless but triumphant, and waddle towards the door. He, too, like an advertisement for Michelin Tyres, waddles beside.

" Hi ! stop. Wait ! "

I halt ; surely I cannot have forgotten anything ? But yes — my parachute ! I sling it over my shoulder and we go into the flight office.

My instructor greets me — " Sorry, old boy, all scrubbed for the moment — bad forecast."

My R.O. and I look at each other. Then we sit down slowly and beg a cigarette. Our own are buried away under layers of clothing almost to our skin.

But finally we may go. I sign the authorisation book, sign for my colour card and we go out. I buckle on my parachute — tight fit with all this on — and my R.O. gives me a leg up. I scramble along to the entrance hatch — which is cocked. I call out to an airman who must crawl up inside and undo it. Inevitably he says . . . before disappearing from view, but he gets it open and I wallow in — my R.O. following, for on this trip he is to sit beside me and work the U/C.

I settle into my bucket seat and together we dig around for the straps. Yesterday's mud has caked hard on — good, at least I shan't get filthy for once. An airman shouts from the darkness outside " Petrol on ! " Damn them. " No, not yet." Why can't they have a little patience ? The straps will not meet. We try to lengthen them, hitting our hands and fumbling with the torch I have pulled out of my boot. But they are fully stretched. Oh well, by now I really don't care. If we do a crash landing, we do a crash landing. If I go through the windscreen, I go through the windscreen. I switch on the petrol — " Petrol on ! " — plug in my R.T. and by screwing sideways in the seat and feeling behind me find the oxygen plug. My R.O. tells me he cannot find his. Again I switch on the torch. There is none. He must do without. I switch the torch off and turn on the ignition.

" Contact starboard."

I strain my eyes through the shoddy, uncleaned perspex, but I can see neither the fitter nor his torch, only the night, starry but very dark, and light against that darkness, furtive clouds hustled before the wind.

"Contact starboard!" I shout again, and reach for the starboard engine starter button, somewhere behind my left ear. This time I see the fitter, but not out in front. He has scrambled up on to the wing and clutching on to the cockpit hood he puts his head in out of the wind.

"Scrubbed again, sir," he says hoarsely, "switch her off."

I curse quietly, automatically, but without conviction, and clambering out stiffly we walk back to the crew room.

"Sorry, old boy, been put to sixty minutes." The O/C night flying fingers his lower lip apologetically, and goes on — "Afraid we'll have to sleep here. There's a gale warning at the moment and 60 below freezing at 10,000 feet, but they expect it to clear up about 3 A.M. If you'll get out of your gear I'm getting some transport and we'll go and get some supper."

Six pilots and their R.O.s climb aboard and we rattle round to the night flying canteen and get some hot sausages and tea.

W., my R.O., settles down beside me and asks me if I'm going to hear the gramophone concert in the R.T. hut the following night. "They're playing Beethoven's Fifth," he adds.

Opposite us sit George, a plug-ugly likeable young Australian animal, and his R.O. — also an Australian. George butts in.

"Just like Pommie to waste his time listening to that *dashing* Beethoven — waste o' time, that's all."

"Why, George?" I ask.

The long thin mouth, close up under a long square nose, splits up into the half-moon that I can never be sure is a smirk or scowl.

" *Dashing* old Hillary," he says with the greatest goodwill. " Want an argument, do yer ? Well, I know a good tune when I hear one. . . . Got an ear for music — but to sit there hearing why a lot of instruments make that noise just because your grandparents tell yer it's good — get *dashing*."

W. leans across to me. " You know, if I ever had any doubts about the Darwinian theory, George has settled them."

George's little pig eyes move restlessly between us ; there is a frown of suspicion on his forehead.

" Come on, George, you old . . ." I say. " What about your argument ? What do you mean by *good* music ? "

George's brow clears. He puts back his head and cackles. " *Dashing* Pommies," he says, and then he tells me about music.

But suddenly I felt quite exhausted. I wasn't trying to be funny or even to get a rise out of George as W. loves to do, but I was quite suddenly unutterably weary of it and merely wished to eat.

" O.K., George," I said. " You win, I can't argue with you."

George looks suspicious again. " Too *dashing* clever for me, that's what you think, isn't it? Too *dashing* civilised. Well, my father kept a Hotel. What do you think of that ? " His face is pushed close to mine. Oh dear, oh dear, oh dear. How did I get pushed into this corner ?

" Probably the man who made his money by pinching our bloody sheep and sending us broke when we had a station," I say. It's all right, George is happy again.

" Boy, what wouldn't I give to be surfing right now on Bondi Beach instead of sitting here *dashing* freezing."

His R.O. breaks in, his eyes alight. " Yeah, in the hot sun, with no clothes on, getting freckles on your arse."

We all shout with laughter and bang the table. Peace is permanently restored.

" You know," says George, " I like you, Hillary — in spite of all that bull."

I think what an ideal crew George and his R.O. make, and I mentally raise my hat to the Wing Commander. I also ponder Koestler's theory that *l'espoir de la fraternité* is always a wild goose chase unless one is tight or physically exhausted in a crowd — as after long marches.

Tonight I am almost convinced that he is right. But he must not be — for it was for that reason that I returned.

We finished our meal and were driven back in the truck to the crew room at Dispersal where we laid out some blankets, piled up the fire and turned in ; the wind howling and whistling outside and the door bursting open and banging continuously. All the others asleep, so I had to shut it. Woke once and looked at my watch — 6 o'clock — I can still hear the wind and I am not sorry. At 7 o'clock we are shouted at and woken up. Transportation is ready to take us up to the mess. We must have breakfast and be down again at 8.30.

The night is over. The day begins.

★

There came a night at the beginning of the New Year, cold, clear and lit with winking stars.

W. and I clambered into all our equipment and were driven over to A Squadron to pick up No. 238. We only had to try two other A/C before getting the right one in the dark, so we were in not too bad a temper. As there was nothing for him to do on a height test W. sat up in front with me. We plugged in our oxygen and turned it on full, squeezing the tubes to see if it was coming through. Mine seemed O.K. — his also. We taxied out — always a nightmare to me as I cannot reach the brake — and last night a 40 m.p.h. cross wind.

The serviceability rate of these A/C is so low that I always marvel whenever we leave the ground at all. But anything goes here and off we went. As soon as we were off the ground, I knew something was wrong. The old monster started plunging away to starboard. We flashed a torch through the filthy perspex to see if the gills had not shut, but they seemed O.K. so I continued. (I wonder if W. knows just how terrified I am at night? I hope not.) Then we started to climb. At 10,000 ft. the pitch control of the port engine jammed. At 19,000 I was waffling about at 100 m.p.h. with the outside temperature 50 below. Then the R.T. packed up (I could receive from the ground but not transmit).

I told W. to get a homing. I listened to him calling up — his voice very drowsy. Oh God, he's going to pass out! Down I pushed the nose, down until I thought my ears would crack — all the time hearing ground control giving us homing vectors and W. repeating them, slowly, happily and quite wrong. I should of course have kept a mental note of the course we were flying, but having so much to do I had left it to W. What if the R.T. packs up altogether? A moment later it did so. A feeling, oddly enough of resignation — not panic. Then I saw it, — the flare path, way below us. We were all right. I came down slowly, feeling very sick (my own supply of oxygen cannot have been very good), and started to reflash my navigation lights at 1,000 ft. Nothing happened. Why the Hell couldn't they answer ? I glanced again at my instruments. 11,000 ft. ! What a fool — must get down. That might have led to disaster — a quick circuit at what I took to be 1,000 ft. ; turn nicely over, the East funnel of lights at 800 ft. — wheels down, flaps down, throttle back down to 100 ft. Why no chance light ? — and then the stall. Too late I realise what has happened. We are not at 10,000 ft. and all the time the plane is spinning and spinning.

Well that's what might have been. Another lesson learned.

I lose more height and when I am at 800 ft. start flashing my navigation lights. A green lamp flashes back. I can land. I turn to W. and put up my thumb. He grins back, quite unaware that he was nearly out. (He has great confidence in me ! If he did but know !)

Round the circuit and down with my wheels — a flood of light comes on where the ground crew have not put strips over the undercarriage pointive indicator lights. I am quite blinded, but W. gets down on his knees and holds his hand over the glare.

We are coming in. Hell of a cross wind, — we're drifting badly. I straighten up over the runway, throttle back, wings still going like a crab. Then the wheels touch and we are down. As I turn off the runway I can feel the sweat running down inside my Irving suit and my hands are trembling. Climbing out I put my foot gingerly to the ground. Oh, how welcome it is. Solid earth beneath my feet.

In the air twice I had promised myself that if I got down I should go to the Wing Commander and say that I'd had enough. Already the mere thought of it amused me.

What was for supper? That occupied the first place in my mind.

We staggered back to the crew room, weighed down by our parachutes, fears forgotten, chattering and laughing.

We were met by the Officer I/C night flying — the M.O. and an ambulance.

"What has happened? Are you all right?"

"Yes," I said. "My R.T. packed up and Fison was answering for me. He doesn't know the patter, that's all. Actually, two supply was a little short, I think."

"Oh, that's what happened. We thought you'd had it."

Grinning with relief they start up the ambulance and offer us a cigarette. I took one from the M.O. wondering what he'd think if he knew how very nearly I had made use of that ambulance, said I was ill, sick at altitude, anything. Nobody could blame me. There was still time. W. helped me out of my kit, I relit my cigarette and we walked over to night supper.

Then no transport — somebody had boobed again and so the long, weary, cold walk up to the mess. Time, midnight.

Outside I bade W. goodnight (how much rather that he were allowed in our mess than some of the others) and walked in for a moment before going to bed.

A party was going on. I could hear a piano playing and a huge barrel of beer frothed past, carried by four drunken clowns. I collected some letters from my locker and turned to go to my room. But one of them saw me — my Flight Commander.

"What ho, Heil! How did it go?"

I told him. He answered quite soberly. "Christ, old boy, shaky do, eh? I wouldn't fly one of these Blenheims at night for any price. I tried it once — shook me to the tits — can't ever see the instruments and *dashing* all outside. Oh, it's a grand life we lead here, old boy. Tomorrow you'll have all that and your engine'll cut too just for full measure, and if you prang they'll say it was your fault. Come on in, someone's birthday — good excuse for getting pissed — only thing to do here."

★

On the night of January 7th the sky was again wintry, but this time the stars were only fleetingly visible when the wintry wind with sudden fierceness broke the wall of cloud, and for a minute or two showed the immense distance that lay behind.

The flight he made before midnight was without incident. He and Walter Fison, his navigator, went back to the hut and crouched over the stove. They did not take their heavy equipment off, for there was time only for a cigarette and a cup of tea before having to make a second flight.

Occasional sleet was falling as they rose above the aerodrome after midnight. They were told by radio-telephone to circle a flashing beacon. The heavy machine clove the night and, "Are you happy?" the telephone asked. "Moderately," came back Richard's voice to the ground. "I am continuing to orbit."

The officer on the ground watched the machine slowly circling, its port wing tilted towards the beacon.

Then, " My God," he said, " he's losing height."

Urgently the voice on the ground called the plane, but there was no reply. Lower and lower, with great widening sweeps, the Blenheim came towards the earth, the navigation lights drawing frightening arcs against the night sky.

*

From the smouldering wreckage little was rescued that identified Richard Hillary and Walter Fison. Annihilation was now complete. The charred bodies were brought home for burial, and from their lockers the solemn secrets of these young lives were gathered up, checked by the Effects Officer, and returned to their relatives.

Richard's cigarette case was found on his body.

> Cigarette case, gold, with initials and inscription, one. Documents : pages of a diary [The Security Officers carefully scrutinized these for security reasons, both at Charter Hall and at Whitehall] ; last will and testament, one.

This last document is in Richard's authentic voice. After disposing of his property, it read : " I want no one to go into mourning for me. As to whether I am buried or cremated, it is immaterial to me, but as the flames have had one try, I suggest they might get their man in the end.

" I want no one to feel sorry for me. In an age

when no one can make a decision that is not dictated from above, it was left to me to make the most important decision of all. . . . In my life I had a few friends, I learnt a little wisdom and a little patience. What more could a man ask for ? "

★

The next night Sergeant-Pilot Miller sat writing to his parents, " feeling pretty badly ". A copy of the letter was sent by his mother to Edwyna Hillary, and in her letter endorsing it Mrs. Miller wrote—" A Mother's lot from the moment she gives life to her son is to sacrifice for him ".

Dear Mom and Pop,

Dick Hillary was killed early Friday morning, and as I saw it done I feel pretty badly about it. We had had supper together that night before going up. I had been up once, and was detailed to go up again, but as I got a severe icing I returned to base. In the meantime Hillary had gone up. All at once, as I was about to change, I heard a whine and a terrific crash. I said, " Christ, I hope that isn't Hillary." I ran to the officer. He rushed out — [had] telephoned 102 [who] had not answered. My God, it was Hillary.

I hope you will excuse this short note, but I don't feel like writing any more.

Your loving son,

Handel.

Requiem

A SOCIETY called The Association of Combatant Writers, its members composed of those who fought in the Resistance, meets once a year in Paris to honour the memory of some writer who fell in the battle for liberty. Since the war they have celebrated in successive years the memory of a Dane, Kajmunk, of a Norwegian, Nordhal-Grieg, and a Belgian, Auguste Marin. This year, 1950, they honoured Richard Hillary, and at a most moving ceremony in Paris on May the 20th, nearly ten years after the Battle of Britain, a requiem was held for the man who has been the subject of this memoir. The hall in which the ceremony was held was crowded, and in the presence of Richard's mother and father, speeches honouring their son were made by the President of the Association, the British Ambassador, General de Larminat, Mlle. Jeanne Bortel, of the Comédie Française, and the Marquis de Amodo. Since what was said of him came from those who had not known him, from men, some prominent in the affairs of the world, and from others not now famous, but who, in the relentless, nerve-racking struggle of the Resistance, had kept their courage and had survived, the witness they then bore to Richard's virtues may stand as a worthier epitaph than any I can write.

M. Pierre Chanlaine :

If the passionate love of a life of pleasure, of enjoyment, saps the energy of a man, and prepares him for every kind of compromise and weakness, as history constantly testifies, what pride it must be for a nation to count among its ranks young men like the author of this book.

Richard Hillary reminds us of Saint-Exupéry. These two men appear to us as knights of the present day, as crusaders without a cross, who have striven by their accounts to exalt the constant and often unknown efforts of their comrades, to serve a cause which to them seemed great, crusaders whom death had magnified until it gave to their memory the semblance of divinity.

We who have fought without weakening because we loved our country, and because we could not bear to live without that precious thing, liberty, we render deeply-felt homage to this young comrade, killed at the age of 22, in the full flowering of his talent.

The British Ambassador to France, Sir Oliver Harvey :

As your President has said, our Richard Hillary reminds us of your Saint-Exupéry. Both were aviators, both were writers. Both lost their lives in the sky, fighting against the same enemy. It is true that between them there are obvious and deep differences, for Saint-Exupéry was an older man who had a much longer experience of flying and of life, he was the author of a number of wonderful books and master of a precise and considered style, while Richard Hillary, killed at the age of 22, left only this one book, in which it is evident that a sincerity of despair, and an uncompromising search into the deep meaning of things, fought hard to find expression. And yet there is a profound similarity between these two men, a similarity derived precisely from this particular quality of sincerity and enquiry. These were men of an extreme sensibility — possessing in fact the sensibility of an artist — forced nevertheless by an interior power to choose action ; two men of action incapable by themselves of finding a happy oblivion in action, because they were tormented by a sense of responsibility and the need to try to understand. This makes of young Richard Hillary, as of Saint-Exupéry, a symbol of the youth of our time in our two countries and beyond their frontiers.

Arthur Koestler has said that Richard Hillary was the embodiment of those " unbelieving crusaders " sick of a " nostalgia for a cause to defend, which nevertheless does not exist " ; " desperate crusaders in search of a Cross ". M. Jean Schlumberger, for his part, in a moving tribute to Hillary's book in its French version, has written : " When I read the beautiful autobiography *The Last Enemy*, I thought of Henri Ghéon . . . the author, Richard Hillary, declares himself in the same way *a man born of war*. . . . Happy those few who, amid the immense destruction, will have been able, like these two, to put against the achievements of death the testimony of a new birth."

The youth of our two countries is tormented by fundamental questions, in a manner which I think is without precedent in history. In particular, war is no longer the simple thing it appeared to be a few generations ago ; but with you as with us, a new testing. I do not think there is any more moving spectacle in the whole of history than that of the courage filled with doubt of our age — the spectacle of the young people of our two profoundly civilized countries, who have never hesitated to look their doubts in the face and go into action. That is why *The Last Enemy*, like Saint-Exupéry's *War-time Pilot*, is a book which will always be read.

Finally, General de Larminat spoke of those soldiers he had known, the descendants of those who had built up the British Empire :

Valiant, strong, skilful, such among them was this young prince of the mind and of the heart, Richard Hillary. He chose that form of combat which was most obvious, most direct, and applied to it his strength, his enthusiasm and his clear-mindedness. In it he served his country well, for it he suffered the acutest pain without complaint, he blithely faced a heroic death.

One of our young parachute troops, Zirnfeld, an Alsatian, killed in action in September 1942, had written these lines :

" I address myself to you, O God,
For you give me
That which one can only obtain from oneself.
Give me, O God, what you have left,
Give me that for which no one ever asks you.
I do not ask for rest
Or tranquillity,
Neither of the soul nor of the body.
I do not ask for wealth
Or success, not even for health.
All these things, O God, you are so often asked for them,
That you must not have any left by now.

Give me, O God, what is left,
Give me that which others refuse.
I want insecurity and anxiety,
I want torment and clashes,
And I want you to give me them, O God,
Once and for all.
I want to be sure to have them always,
For I shall not always have the courage
To ask you for them.
Give me, O God, what you have left,
Give me what others do not want.
But give me also courage,
And strength and faith.
For you are the only one who gives
That which one can only obtain from oneself."

Is it not a similar prayer which emerges from Richard Hillary's book, in which he describes with pitiless lucidity his life as a fighter, the martyrdom of his great injury? Knowing the price to pay, measuring the effort required, he wanted to be, as he wrote at the end of his book, one of those who would continue to fight until the ideal for which their comrades in arms had died had put its seal for ever on the future of civilization.

General de Larminat closed his discourse with these words:

The sacrifice of the élite is a cruel thing, yet without this willingness to sacrifice they would not be the élite, and a Nation is built on its élite. Thank God, those to whom Great Britain gave birth did not fail either her or civilization. Let us bow low and ponder this lesson, both as soldiers and as citizens.

PRINTED BY R. & R. CLARK, LTD., EDINBURGH